BUDDHISM

THE
ELEMENT
LIBRARY

BUDDHISM

JOHN SNELLING

ELEMENT

Shaftesbury, Dorset

Rockport, Massachusetts

Brisbane, Queensland

© Element Books Limited 1996
Text © Sarah Snelling

Published in Great Britain 1996 by
ELEMENT BOOKS LIMITED
SHAFTESBURY, DORSET SP7 8BP

Published in the USA in 1996 by
ELEMENT INC
PO Box 830, Rockport, MA 01966

Published in Australia in 1996 by
ELEMENT BOOKS LIMITED for
JACARANDA WILEY LIMITED
33 Park Road, Milton, Brisbane, 4046

Designed and created by
THE BRIDGEWATER BOOK COMPANY
Art Director *Peter Bridgewater*
Designer *Jane Lanaway*
Editor *Joanne Jessop*
Managing Editor *Anne Townley*
Picture Research *Vanessa Fletcher*
Page Make-up *Chris Lanaway*

Printed in Hong Kong by
Midas Printing Ltd

British Library Cataloguing-in-Publication Data available

Library of Congress Cataloging-in-Publication
Data available

ISBN 1–85230–798–6

CONTENTS

INTRODUCTION • *page 6*

1
SHAKYAMUNI BUDDHA • *page 10*

2
INDIAN BUDDHISM • *page 18*

3
THE BUDDHIST DIASPORA • *page 26*

4
WISDOM 1: THE BASIC TEACHINGS • *page 34*

5
WISDOM 2: MAHAYANA DEVELOPMENTS • *page 44*

6
MORALITY • *page 54*

7
MEDITATION • *page 58*

8
THE PRINCIPAL SCHOOLS AND TRADITIONS • *page 70*

ENDWORD: GOING FURTHER • *page 90*

NOTES AND REFERENCES • *page 93*

ACKNOWLEDGEMENTS • *page 93*

GLOSSARY • *page 94*

FURTHER READING • *page 94*

INDEX • *page 96*

ART CENTER COLLEGE OF DESIGN

INTRODUCTION

Origins of Buddhism

Buddhism is a jewel from the treasure-house of Indian spirituality. It emerged about 2,500 years ago in the central plain of the River Ganges, just south of the Himalayas, which, in all their snowy grandeur, stand as soaring symbols of the spiritual aspirations of the human race. Over the centuries Buddhism has been transmitted to many other countries and in the process has absorbed much of local tradition and undergone exciting new phases of development, but its Indian elements have always remained central and fundamental.

The established form of religion prevalent in India 2,500 years ago was Brahminism. Here a privileged caste of priests mediated between the ordinary people and the gods by controlling specialized religious rites. This tradition – the Vedas were its holy writings – was largely the creation of the dynamic Aryan people who invaded India during the first millennium BCE, though it also drew upon indigenous elements.

Buddhism, on the other hand, emerged from an alternative and rather different religious stream, the origins of which predate the Aryan invasion. This is an ancient yogic tradition, originally without professional priesthood or formal organization, which places primary emphasis on direct personal penetration of the ultimate mysteries of life.

Since time immemorial pious Indians have venerated those spiritual seekers who have gone off alone into the tangled mountains and untamed jungles to discover truth for themselves. A sophisticated spiritual technology evolved to meet their needs: special yogas and meditation practices that, if correctly and diligently applied, might open the eye of wisdom and reveal Ultimate Reality, which is always sought within – in the human heart. Archaeologists digging in the ruins of the cities of the Indus Valley, Mohenjo Daro and Harappa, which had crumbled into the dust long before the first Aryan crossed the Indus, found very ancient images of such yogis sitting cross-legged in the lotus posture.

Although originally unsystematic and anarchic, around 600 BCE some groups of yogis, who had gathered around particular teachers or shramana, began to feel the need to present a more coherent and organized face to the world. At the time an economic revolution was under way in the middle Ganges region. New prosperity had created bustling commercial towns and cities populated by classes of *nouveaux riches* who had both the leisure and inclination for philosophical and religious inquiry. The Buddha was just such a teacher, and it was proverbially from among the 'young men of good family' that he drew many of his first disciples. Of the other shramana groups originally active, the only other one that survives today is the Nigrantha or Jains: the followers of Mahavira.

INDIVIDUAL TRUTH

Every great religion is founded by what we might call a spiritual original, one of those exceedingly rare individuals graced with the courage and vision to venture into the labyrinth of themselves and penetrate the great mystery enshrined at its core. Such a person knows truth for himself, not at second hand, having drunk at the living source.

Afterwards he may teach others, but at once problems arise. Firstly, disciples usually do not possess the spiritual talent of their masters; and secondly, there is a limit to what can be taught anyway, for each individual is unique, an entirely new configuration, and must in the last analysis find his or her own way to the centre.

The death of a master will inevitably present a special crisis. His teachings will be formalized and written down. In time they will become ossified and lifeless. Priesthood and hierarchy will assert themselves, and a worldly structure will orchestrate itself, attracting wealth and power, which leads to rivalry, schism, careerism, dogmatism and so forth.

It would be naïve and dishonest to pretend that the religion of Buddhism, as it was developed by other men and women after the death of the Buddha, did not fall into some of the pitfalls described above. However, the Buddha himself was very much concerned, not with offering dogmatic formulations, but with helping people to see the Truth and find liberation for themselves. So elemental to all his teachings is what we might call a liberal spirit of free inquiry. This spirit is clearly expressed in the *Kalama Sutta*, which describes how the Buddha visited the Kalamas, a clan living in the environs of the city of Kesaputta. After the usual formalities, the Kalamas told him:

Certain holy men and brahmin priests come to Kesaputta and teach. As for the teachings of others, they mock them. Then others come and do the same thing. As a result, whenever we listen to holy men and priests, we are full of doubt and waver in uncertainty as to who is speaking truth, who falsehood.

The Buddha replied unequivocally:

Yes, Kalamas, you may well doubt and waver in uncertainty. But do not be misled by report or hearsay or what is stated on the authority of your traditional teachings. Do not be misled by those proficient in quoting scripture, nor by logic or inference, nor after reflection on mere opinion or theory, nor blindly out of a respect for a holy man or priest. Only when you know for yourselves: such teachings are good, they cause no harm, they are accepted by the wise, when performed they produce positive benefits and happiness — then, Kalamas, you may accept and abide in them ...

The crucial words here are *only when you know for yourselves*. The Buddha was certainly not trying to peddle the Kalamas just another religion or ideology, however noble. He was pointing to something in themselves: a timeless inner centre of wisdom. And with that wisdom invariably goes a warm and kindly compassion for others who are caught in the net of suffering.

For those who need them, all the usual consolations of religion are on offer in Buddhism. One can opt to be a believer, a person of faith and pious devotion. But the main call has always been for the individual to follow the Buddha's example and wake up to knowledge of the Truth for himself (or herself – this is understood throughout), in his own unique way. This is what makes Buddhism so relevant to our times and why it is attracting such a large following in the West today. Westerners have had enough of organized religion and its products and effects. Right now we need more spirit, more direct knowledge: to drink of the living waters. Indeed, we deeply thirst for it.

BELOW *A mandala of the state of exalted consciousness.*

SHAKYAMUNI
BUDDHA

*D espite the many developments through which the religious tradition that bears his
name has gone, the historical Buddha remains fundamental. He is the founding
genius, the hero, the trail-blazer. Yet, for all that, the Buddha remains a shadowy figure, though
Buddhist hagiography has enlarged his life story and embellished it with a baroque complexity of
miraculous and marvellous detail. He was apparently born around 566 BCE into a leading
family of one of the small tribal republics that had sprung up in northern India. The domains of
his people, the Shakyas, were situated right beneath the Himalayan foothills, part of them in
what today would fall within the Nepalese Terai. Consequently he is sometimes called
Shakyamuni, the 'Sage of the Shakyas'; his personal name was Siddhartha Gautama.*

THE EARLY YEARS

Legend has it that soon after Siddhartha was born he was scrutinized by Asita, a holy man with paranormal powers. Asita foretold that Siddhartha would become either a great world leader or a great religious teacher. This somewhat dismayed the child's father, Shuddhodana, who wanted to see him follow in his own privileged footsteps. Reasoning that it would be experience of the hard side of life that would turn young Siddhartha's mind towards religion, Shuddhodana created a hermetic environment of pleasure and luxury for his son. Consequently the boy grew up knowing little of the realities of life, though by all accounts he was superabundantly gifted with talents and graces, as well as being very high-minded.

In due course, Siddhartha blossomed into a kind of story-book hero and married a beautiful wife, Yashodhara. However, around the time that his one and only son, Rahula, was born, curiosity about conditions in the outside world began to nibble away at him. He was perhaps growing dissatisfied with the mere happiness of life in his marble palace-prisons with their beautiful gardens and pools, bored with the courtesans and dancers and musicians that were laid on at all times to amuse him, tired of lounging around in fine silks and dining on only the daintiest of delicacies.

Shuddhodana responded by arranging for Siddhartha to be driven down to the local village, but he first ordered that all people with any kind of disability be kept out of sight so as not to upset the prince's sensitive nature. The arrangements miscarried, however, for on the first three visits that Siddhartha made to the village he saw things that had a deeply traumatic effect on his over-protected consciousness. He was, in short, summarily initiated into the reality of suffering in three of its most poignant forms: old age, sickness and death. Realizing, apparently for the first time, that he too must one day be subject to those fates, he became at once dark and withdrawn. Even in his palaces – *especially* in his palaces – life was no longer tenable.

Then, on a fourth drive to the village, Siddhartha met a sadhu or holy man: one of those ragged ascetics, perhaps with long beard and tangled hair, who still walk the hot and dusty roads of India with no belongings or money, depending on the kindness of other people for their support. Yet this homeless mendicant possessed a certain air of calmness and a nobility of bearing that suggested to Siddhartha that he had come to terms with old age, sickness and death.

So a point of crisis was reached. The outcome was that Siddhartha left his palaces. He gave up wealth and privilege. He even hacked off his handsome jet-black hair and exchanged his fine silk robes for the ragged ones of a holy man. Then he too wandered off into the world, alone and unsupported, to find an answer to the problem of suffering, which would be the same as finding a path to liberation from the painful rounds of cyclic existence. He was then about 29.

OPPOSITE *The Shakyas' tribal republic, into which the Buddha was born, was situated beneath the Himalayan foothills.*

BELOW *A Buddhist monument in Java, Indonesia, showing a scene from the early life of the Buddha.*

THE SPIRITUAL QUEST

LEFT *Setting out on his path to Enlightenment, Siddhartha gave up all his possessions and even cut off his long black hair.*

Siddhartha spent the next few years (536–532) on an intensive spiritual quest. In jungle retreats, he studied first at the feet of Alara Kalama, one of the foremost yogic teachers of his day. Alara taught him methods of deep meditation that led to a very high and subtle dhyana or state of trance. A model student, Siddhartha applied himself whole-heartedly to the practice and achieved realization. Delighted, Alara offered to promote him to the status of fellow teacher, but Siddhartha declined. This teaching, he reflected, would not lead to total release from suffering but only to protracted sojourn on the Plane of Nothingness. So he went to Udraka Ramaputra, another foremost yogic teacher, and, with similar dedication, absorbed and practised his teachings, only to come finally to the same conclusion as before, but this time the result would be a sojourn on the Plane of Neither Perception or Non-Perception.

At this point Siddhartha had come to two important realizations. Firstly, he discovered that concentrative meditation (shamatha practice – this is described in greater detail in Chapter 7) does not lead to complete liberation; something else is required. And, secondly, he saw that there inevitably comes a point where teachers can teach us no more. Then, however painful the parting, we have to move on, no longer reaching out to external sources for wisdom but seeking that true source in our own heart centre.

So Siddhartha left Udraka Ramaputra and tried to find his own way. Initially he experimented with extreme ascetic practices: living in graveyards, sleeping on beds of thorns, frying in the noonday heat and freezing beneath the moon at night, he starved and punished his body in the hope that in that way he could root out all desire. Again, he applied himself so wholeheartedly that he attracted an admiring circle of five fellow yogis. He also brought himself to the verge of death. Then, at the eleventh hour, terminally weak and emaciated, he realized that he had still not found what he was looking for and would probably die if he persisted. So he abandoned his austerities and took a little food, a lapse that so disgusted the five yogis that they declared, 'Siddhartha has taken to the easy life!' – and promptly abandoned him.

THE BODHI TREE

Quite alone now, a man *in extremis*, Siddhartha sat himself on a cushion of kusha grass beneath a peepul tree – the Bo or Bodhi Tree – at a place called Bodhgaya, which lies in the modern Indian state of Bihar. He was determined to sit on that 'immovable spot' until he found an answer to his problem ... or die in the attempt.

Siddhartha's spiritual quest reached its climax beneath the Bodhi Tree on the night of the full moon of May. Years before, when as a young boy he had been left beneath a tree during the Ploughing Festival that the Shakyas celebrated each spring, he had closed his eyes and fallen into an introverted state of meditation. He now repeated that process and began an in-depth exploration of his own inner being. Much repressed or subconscious material must have 'come up' – as modern meditators say: dark fears, erotic fantasies, self-indulgent impulses, fragments of memory – but he did not allow himself to be distracted by it. Instead, by watching his own mental movie-show with cool alertness, he was able to neutralize its seductive power and its contents thereby passed away.

ABOVE *A modern-day Buddhist monk, as the Buddha before him, meditates under a bodhi tree in search of Enlightenment.*

ENLIGHTENMENT

Persisting in concentration, Siddhartha's mind became as calm and bright as a mirror, so that he was able to have clear insight into the basic mechanisms that create and sustain Samsara. He relived his own innumerable past births in the different ages of the world – ages of expansion and ages of dark contraction. Then, turning his attention to others, he saw how they circulated through the cycles of birth and death, and that the way in which they passed on was determined by the moral quality of their actions (karma). He then considered how the 'defilements' (sensual desire, ignorance and so on) that cause suffering could be extirpated and, seeing that it was indeed possible to do so, he was himself freed. He lastly surveyed the twelve links of the chain of Dependent Origination, which in effect describe how birth inevitably leads, by way of a series of predictable stages, to death, which is a prelude to yet another birth – and one that will merely turn the Wheel of Life through another repetitious revolution unless the process is stopped.

Siddhartha must have seen too that he was caught up in this blind, machine-like process himself. If the deep mechanics of his own being were allowed to have their way, the notion of a separate, individual being or person would inevitably arise – in his case, Siddhartha Gautama – a person with a name, history, social rôle, memories, relationships and so on. But this was really a fictional construct. At depth, in its true nature, the reality was very different. He was not simply Siddhartha Gautama at all, but something far more marvellous than that. His true self was in fact vast, open, unconditioned.

Seeing this, an enormous burden slipped away. He was free at last. For it was the person Siddhartha Gautama who was the prisoner of the gyres of the Wheel of Life, sentenced to endless rounds of pleasure and pain, death and rebirth. His true self, however, was beyond the dualities of pain and pleasure, space and time, life and death. This was Nirvana.

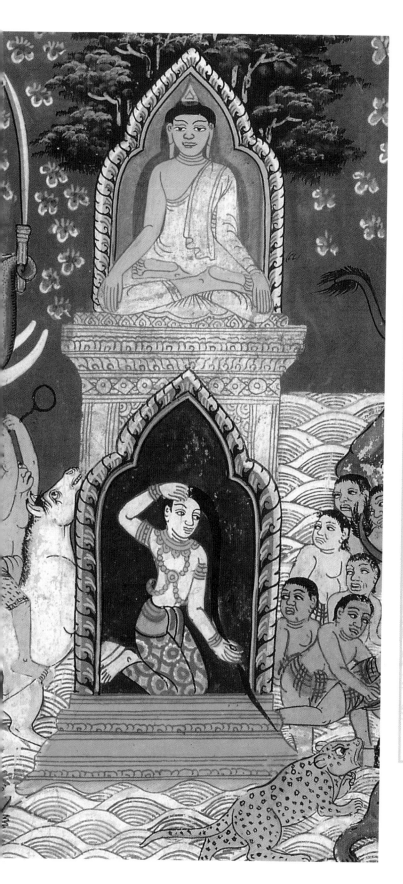

When, towards dawn, Siddhartha looked up, he saw the morning star rise with new eyes – not the eyes of Siddhartha Gautama but those of the Buddha: the 'One Who is Awake', the 'One Who Knows'.

For some time the Buddha continued to sit beneath the Bo Tree, enjoying the supreme bliss of his Enlightenment. He did consider teaching, but at first he held out little hope that his message would meet with a positive reception. Then the idea came to him that there might be some with 'just a little dust in their eyes', who might be liberated if they were approached in the right way.

Rediscovering the Dharma

Buddha's Enlightenment was not merely an event of personal or racial significance but, according to Buddhist hagiography, of cosmic proportions. Some of the more mythically-enriched accounts describe how beings in the heavens and the hells, as though watching from galleries, stalls and auditoria at this momentous event happening at the centre of the world-stage, broke into ecstatic applause. For the Dharma, the Path to Liberation, which had been lost for aeons, had been rediscovered. A vast dark age had been brought to an end. New light and hope had entered the world. Others might become Enlightened; some, the pratyeka-buddhas, keep their wisdom to themselves; but it is specifically the function of buddhas, an apostolic line of whom may be traced back into the mists of the beginningless past with vast gulfs between them, to rediscover the Dharma and proclaim it. Siddhartha Gautama is specifically the buddha of our own age.

LEFT *The earth trembled, testifying to the Buddha's future Enlightenment, after he had defeated the spirit of evil, Mara, who approached him on the elephant Girimekhala.*

THE TEACHING CAREER

So began a 45-year ministry (531–485 BCE) during which the Buddha wandered between the towns, villages and cities of the middle Ganges plain, mainly in the ancient kingdoms of Magadha and Kosala. From the start he seems to have possessed a kind of radiance that stirred a deep response in those who met him. He was also a teacher of consummate skill and, though he never set himself up as a competitive rival to the other religious teachers or to the brahmin priesthood, all the indications are that he was very concerned to get his message across. For one thing, he wished his teachings to be formulated in the local dialects in which they would be fully accessible to ordinary people and not in the rarefied liturgical language of the times. And it is clear from the accounts that large numbers of people, of all classes and conditions, became enlightened by his teachings.

The Buddha's teachings are not merely for intellectual contemplation. They involve practice: things to do – and things requiring discipline and application. Though many of his early followers were lay people, there were also those who wished to give up the world and family life in order to devote their time and energy entirely to the Dharma. So emerged the Sangha, the community of Buddhist monks, to which later nuns were admitted. At first the Sangha lived lives of extreme simplicity as homeless mendicants, dressing in rags, living only on alms-food and seeking shelter in caves and beneath the roots of trees. Later, however, thanks to the largesse of wealthy lay benefactors – the Buddha numbered among his devotees kings, aristocrats and rich merchants – they obtained more permanent and comfortable residences during the Monsoon or Rainy Season. These were the beginnings of vihare: Buddhist monasteries.

Such was the purity and power of the Buddha's message that, at first, the Sangha needed no rules to regulate its life. Gradually, however, occasioned by specific lapses, a code of rules, the Pratimoksha, was evolved for monks and nuns, as were principles of government, which were highly democratic. The Buddha, it seems, never sought to set himself up as an authority figure or reduce his disciples to the state of blind followers. Nevertheless, internal dissension did arise within the Sangha and, on one occasion, the Buddha withdrew in disgust at the quarrelsome antics of some of his monks. The only really serious schism, however, was fomented by his cousin, Devadatta.

BELOW *Buddhist monks in India. Modern monks, like those during the time of the Buddha, give up family life in order to devote themselves entirely to the Dharma.*

THE FINAL YEAR

Comparatively detailed accounts exist of the last year of the Buddha's life. As usual, he wandered from place to place, giving wise and compassionate teachings. He died around 486 BCE, when he was about 80 years old. His last words to his disciples were a pithy encapsulation of his whole teaching:

Impermanent are all created things. Strive on with awareness.

Then he passed into Parinirvana, an ineffable state utterly beyond the scope of ordinary mental comprehension or verbal description.

This again was an event of cosmic significance. Great anguish was felt and expressed in all six 'destinations' — for a buddha, a fully enlightened one who rediscovers and proclaims the Dharma after it has been lost during a vast dark age, appears in the world only very, very rarely indeed.

LEFT *The Parinirvana — the state Enlightened beings enter after physical death — of the Buddha.*

INDIAN BUDDHISM

Buddhism has not been a significant religious presence in India for many hundreds of years. But it did thrive in the subcontinent for over 1,000 years after the death of its originating genius. During that period it underwent many important developments. With hindsight we can trace the emergence of three major traditions or new 'turnings of the wheel of the Dharma'.

1: BASIC BUDDHISM *(Hinayana or 'Little Vehicle')*

The Buddha was a dynamic spiritual master teacher who gave out teachings according to the demands of specific situations. Though, by virtue of his attainment, he possessed a certain natural authority, which was apparently quite self-evident (according to accounts he possessed a golden radiance), he never tried to set himself up as a leader figure, nor did he nominate a successor. He obviously wished to inculcate self-reliance in his followers and avoid all the pitfalls that go with

power and authority. He just indicated that, if there was a need for guidance after his death, his followers might look to his Dharma, his teachings.

Soon after his death and cremation, however, the Buddha's monks and nuns came together from the far-flung regions where they had gravitated and held a great council, the first of several, at which the teachings were orally rehearsed. An 'authorized version' was eventually, but not without some

difficulty, agreed upon. It was then committed to memory by specialists and transmitted by word of mouth for more than 400 years. A written version was not produced until the first century CE in Sri Lanka. This huge body of scriptures is called the Pali Canon after its medium, Pali, one of the ancient dead languages of India. An alternative name is Tripitaka (Tipitaka in Pali) or 'Three Baskets', on account of its trivision into three main sections of the scripture.

'Three Baskets' of the Pali Canon

The Pali Canon, also known as the Tripitaka, was divided into three main sections or 'baskets':
1 The Vinaya Pitaka or Basket of Discipline, which includes the code of rules by which monks and nuns should live, plus other materials.
2 The Sutra Pitaka or Basket of Teachings: the collections of long, middle-length, short and other instructional discourses of the Buddha.
3 The Abhidharma Pitaka or Basket of Higher Teachings. The compilers of Abhidharma extracted and systematized the basic philosophical ideas implicit in the Buddha's teachings.

In a way all this repeats a familiar pattern. A great spiritual master emerges, imparts his wisdom to his followers in an *ad hoc* manner, then goes the way of all flesh. He may even declare, like the great modern sage J Krishnamurti, that 'there are no teachings' and that 'truth is a trackless land'. But still there always seems an urge to capture and fix the letter of his utterances. Can their spirit, which after all is the heart of the matter, be caught, though? And if there is more reliance on letter than on spirit, is there not a danger of fundamentalism: of applying in life situations not the wisdom of the heart, but hoary precedents enshrined in venerable writ?

In the case of the Pali Canon there are also these matters to consider. The Buddha's original teachings were certainly not given in Pali, or in Sanskrit, the high priestly language of ancient India, but in some other lost demotic language, probably Magadhi, the language of the kingdom of Magadha. They were then retailed by his followers during their missionary activities in other parts of India in a variety of other demotic languages. And moreover, not all those present at their original council agreed with what they heard but held to their own variant versions. Furthermore, during the 400-year oral phase there must have been great latitude for small changes to creep in: insertions and deletions – for the best possible reasons, of course.

So, while it might be tempting to regard parts of the Pali Canon as Buddhavacana, the Word of the Buddha, it would perhaps be a little unwise as well as contrary to the non-fundamentalist spirit of Buddhism to do so. The wisest course would rather be to read and study the scriptures with an open mind, one that is both appreciative and critical, with a view, not so much to fixing a literal understanding in one's mind, but of imbibing the underlying spirit.

By and large, the story during this early period was mainly one of success, and that was in part due to the fact that Buddhism still no doubt retained a great deal of its original impetus and vitality despite all attempts to organize it into a religion. It also enjoyed the patronage of powerful rulers, notably the Emperor Ashoka (third century BCE), who underwent a dramatic conversion after witnessing the terrible carnage produced by one of his campaigns. This transformed him from a conventional war-mongering monarch into an enlightened man of peace, concerned not to enlarge or enrich his Indian empire but to raise the moral standards of his people. It is unclear, however, whether Ashoka actually embraced Buddhism or was just highly sympathetic to it.

OPPOSITE *Buddhist temples dating from the seventh and eighth centuries at the Ellora caves north-east of Bombay, India.*

BELOW *A wall painting in Sri Lanka showing Princess Sangamitta. Sangamitta, the daughter of Emperor Ashoka, and her brother, Mahinda, were ordained members of a Sangha and introduced Buddhism to Sri Lanka.*

2 : MAHAYANA *('Great vehicle')*

The Buddha himself foresaw that his teachings would, by stages, lose their vitality and effectiveness. However, by skilfully leaving things flexible and open-ended, he allowed for new waves of creativity and development periodically to revitalize the tradition that he had set going. The first of these waves was the Mahayana, the so-called Great Vehicle.

The Rise of Mahayana

The word Mahayana is really a kind of portmanteau term that embraces a whole range of different dispositions and developments that began to arise among the Buddhist faithful a few hundred years after the Buddha's death. These were definitely *Buddhist*; that is, their proponents primarily revered the Buddha and adhered to his basic teachings as well as the goal of Enlightenment. But they also represented the blossoming of hidden potentials that had hitherto lain latent within the tradition. They may have been

BELOW A monk from Ladakh, India. The Mahayana tradition spread out to the north, to India, Nepal and Tibet.

Nagarjuna, a second-century sage, claimed the authority of Mahayana doctrine by producing the Prajñaparamita, which he claimed had been composed by the Buddha himself and then hidden away in the custody of the Naga demigods until humanity was sufficiently enlightened to comprehend so abstruse a system.

initiated in one place, but they may equally well have arisen synchronously in different locations at more or less the same time. Various non-Buddhist influences, perhaps even ones from the West, may also have encouraged their emergence.

Over centuries these developments began to be associated with a definite movement whose members consciously thought of themselves as Mahayanists as opposed to their precursors, whom they rather disparagingly dubbed 'Hinayanists'. However, as good and tolerant Buddhists, the followers of both traditions must by and large have understood that they were united in something larger than their differences. So, though some sectarian acrimony and division may have taken place, coexistence was possible. We know from the reports of travellers, for instance, that, even as late as the eighth century CE, both Mahayanists and Hinayanists were living side by side in the same monasteries in India.

The Mahayana Buddha

In the Mahayana, the Buddha is seen as the manifestation of a supramundane principle rather than as a flesh-and-blood person. In order to appear as he has in many different realms and times, 'he' has three wonderful bodies at his disposal:

1 the Nirmanakaya, the body in which he appears in the world (though this is not a 'real' body but a magical conjuration for compassionate purposes)

2 the Sambhogakaya, in which he appears in the celestial realms to teach bodhisattvas and their ilk

3 the Dharmakaya, a kind of cosmic body cognate with the Absolute Dharma, the quintessence of Buddha-qualities, the consummation of Shunyata (Emptiness). The historical Buddha is also now often called Tathagata: he who has realized 'thusness' or 'suchness' (tathata).

The Bodhisattva Path

Doctrinally, Mahayanists replace the spiritual ideal of the arhat, the 'noble one' who is assured of Enlightenment, with that of the bodhisattva. The orthodox Mahayana view is that the arhat has attained the salvation of Nirvana for his own benefit alone, and has therefore achieved a lesser and, it is hinted, rather selfish goal. By contrast, the bodhisattva is motivated altruistically. He seeks Nirvana, not for himself, but in order to help others. In this respect he is very much like a buddha – and indeed within the Mahayana the concepts of buddha and bodhisattva seem to blur into each other.

The various bhumi or stages on the Bodhisattva Path are fully charted in the Mahayana, as are the concomitant perfected virtues (paramita). There are six or sometimes ten of these paramita: 1 dana (giving); 2 shila (morality); 3 kshanti (patience); 4 virya (effort); 5 dhyana (meditation); 6 prajña (wisdom); 7 upaya (skill-in-means); 8 pranidhana (resolution); 9 bala (strength); and 10 jñana (knowledge). The faculty of upaya or 'skill-in-means' is strongly stressed, for even a bodhisattva prodigally endowed with compassion would be impotent if he lacked the talent for devising effective ways of translating his good will into practical action. But the paramount Mahayana virtue is compassion (karuna): a warm, even loving concern for others infused with a deep desire to alleviate their suffering. This is elevated alongside wisdom (prajña) as the supreme virtues.

ABOVE *Buddhist teaching is handed down from monk to novice; here amongst the hills of Darjeeling.*

LEFT *A bodhisattva. The bodhisattva is altruistically motivated, seeking Enlightenment in order to help others.*

The Mahayana Pantheon

The Mahayana also spawned a magnificent pantheon of celestial and cosmic buddhas and bodhisattvas, such as Amitabha, the Buddha of Infinite Light, who lives in his Western Paradise of Sukhavati, and Mañjushri, the Bodhisattva of Wisdom, whose adamantine sword slices away false views and delusions. Such developments paved the way for new cults of faith and devotion. Pre-Mahayana Buddhism had been very much focused in the monasteries and concerned with the struggle for Nirvana by personal effort alone. This type of Buddhism was therefore not for the ordinary man but for the educated élite and the dedicated few prepared to renounce the world. Lay people, feeling frustrated or left out, inevitably began to demand a more substantial spiritual status, and these new forms were therefore evolved so that they could express simple faith and could also, aware of their own limitations, call for help from outside agencies.

Mahayana Philosophy and Scriptures

At the other end of the spectrum, for the spiritually sophisticated, new trends and schools of philosophy emerged, all of them highly esoteric. These again undoubtedly emerged to meet real needs. Many of the pre-Mahayana schools of philosophy were losing their edge and beginning to deviate, if only slightly, into the swamps and mires of false views. The new wave of Mahayana philosophers therefore set about devising new philosophical methods and systems that would conduce to right views: that is, views consistent with what the Buddha had actually taught. So these were, in a sense, not so much new philosophies as newly devised upaya or 'skilful means' for arriving at direct perception of old verities. Nor were they systems of pure speculative philosophy as are found in the West but were always linked with meditation practice and so had to point conceptually to the kinds of experience or insight actually gained in the meditation hall.

To get an impression of the vitalizing new energy that the Mahayana unleashed, you have only to look at its vast canon of scriptures. Its texts, often difficult for the modern Westerner to read, are by and large not your everyday book written in plain language and conveying ideas in a logical, coherent form. Rather they are poetically exuberant outpourings from the lofty pinnacle of Enlightenment itself. Amazing things can happen. The reader can be magically transported to the ends of the cosmos, visit infinities of celestial realms encrusted with jewels and suffused with paranormal light, and meet plethoras of buddhas, bodhisattvas and other amazing beings, who perform miraculous feats.

LEFT *Mañjushri, the Bodhisattva of Wisdom, is one of the benign deities.*

RIGHT *Vajrapani, one of the wrathful deities.*

3: VAJRAYANA
(Tantra or 'Thunderbolt Vehicle')

The traveller in India today can still, in certain religious centres, come across that disturbing kind of sadhu or holy man in whom those perennial irreconcilables, asceticism and eroticism, are brought together. He goes about naked, his body smeared with ashes, his beard and hair long and matted, coloured hieroglyphs daubed on his forehead, and a wild, even crazy look in his eyes. This is a tantrika, an adept of Tantra, it is whispered; he frequents charnel grounds and other macabre places, performing unspeakable rites and practices.

Such holy men are spiritual anarchists. They turn the prudent conventions of orthodox religion on their head. Yet, in tolerant India, it has never been denied that their Tantric path is a valid one, even though it may not be suitable for all seekers.

When Mahayana Buddhism in its turn began to lose its first vitality, Tantra entered the Buddhist mainstream and stimulated yet another phase of revitalization and renewal – a third turning of the Wheel of the Dharma. We do not know much about its origins, but by the seventh century CE it had become well established. We now call it Vajrayana[1], the vajra being a Buddhist symbol derived from the mythical thunderbolt of the Indian god Indra: a massive discharge of protean energy that blasts away delusion and inaugurates Enlightenment. It is a very appropriate symbol, for the Tantric path is claimed by its devotees to be a very speedy one, accomplishing in one lifetime what might take countless lifetimes in the Hinayana or Mahayana.

The aim of Tantric practice is to transform one's body, speech and mind into those of a fully enlightened buddha by special yogic means. To this end a variety of ritual and magical methods have been devised, involving the use of specialized forms such as mandala (symbolic models of the cosmos), mantra (sacred formulae) and mudra (hand movements), the bell (ghanta), and the hand-drum (damaru). The power of such things lies in the fact that, in Tantra, everything is invested with cosmic energy. A simple sound may therefore, by virtue of its inherent quantum charge, produce powerful spiritual effects. Practitioners also work with special deities (known in Tibetan as yidam), which may be benign or wrathful but are always imbued with enlightened qualities.

Tantra has its own arcane texts – a 'tantra' is a scripture – but it places primary importance on the guru. He is the guide who can steer the chela or student through the

ABOVE This illustration from an eleventh-century Buddhist manuscript shows Prajñaparamita, the Goddess of Wisdom, flanked by two rows of goddesses and Vajrapani holding a vajra (thunderbolt).

RIGHT The spread of Buddhism has resulted in the creation of vast monastic libraries of texts.

The Tantrikas

Without concrete information, one can only imagine that the earliest Buddhist tantrikas were reminiscent of their colourful modern Hindu counterparts or of the devotees of the old Tantric schools of Tibet – that is, siddhas (adepts), rich in 'crazy wisdom', wandering the world alone or with female consorts, or else married yogis who, in addition to their mystic practices, dispensed occult services – divination, exorcism, rain-making and so on – in their localities. Such people may well have represented, as L O Gomez has written, 'a radical departure from Buddhist monkish prudery' and 'an attempt to shock the establishment out of self-righteous complacency.'[2]

LEFT *The sidhu or holy men who follow the Tantric path in their own unique and eccentric way have always been tolerated in India.*

BELOW *In the Tantric tradition, the bell (ghanta) is an apt simile for the phenomenal world because its sound quickly dies away.*

perilous phantasmagoria of the psycho-spiritual world to the safe shore of Enlightenment. In the eyes of the chela, the guru should appear equal to the Buddha. Tantra is also veiled in secrecy – this has contributed to much confusion about it – and practice cannot begin without the rite of initiation (abhisheka), when the initiate steps into the mandala of his chosen deity.

As might be surmised from the foregoing, what Tantra brought into Buddhism was practical yogic and magical elements. Magic operates, not with the rational mind, but by invoking less developed but no less powerful strata of the psyche (including the emotions and instincts). But inevitably, as the Tantric tradition established itself, steps were taken to sanitize and organize it. It was then monasticized and reconciled with orthodox Buddhist philosophy and practice. Eventually integrated systems were evolved that placed the Vajrayana at the apogee of a three-tiered

hierarchy and the other traditions of Buddhism – the so-called Sutra traditions.

Buddhism gradually went into decline in India after about the seventh century CE. By the thirteenth century it was to all intents and purposes a dead letter. Popular mythology has it that it was the Muslim invasions that destroyed it, or the degenerate influence of Tantra. Yet there were other more significant factors, not least that the ongoing Hindu tradition, with its greater flexibility and involvement with the ordinary life of the people, gained new vitality and reabsorbed much of Buddhism into its own mainstream. Buddhism suffered from being concentrated in the monasteries too, some of which, such as Nalanda and Vikramalashila, had grown into great monastic universities where a whole range of spiritual arts and sciences were taught. When the Muslims did attack, the already weakened Buddhists were easily locatable – and 'liquidatable'.

THE
BUDDHIST DIASPORA

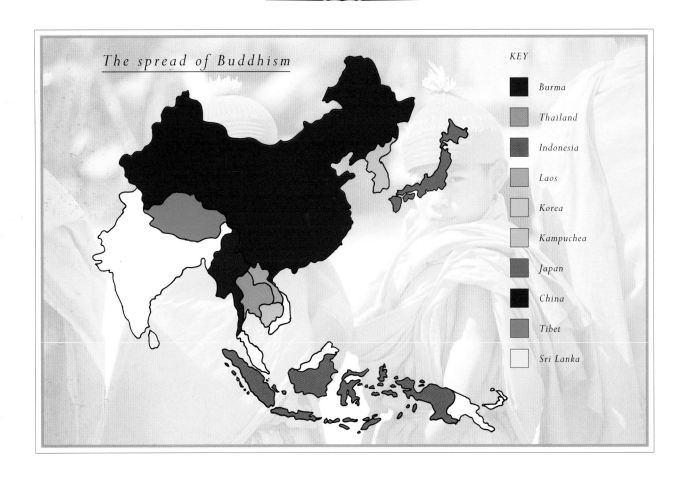

The spread of Buddhism

KEY

- Burma
- Thailand
- Indonesia
- Laos
- Korea
- Kampuchea
- Japan
- China
- Tibet
- Sri Lanka

The decline and fall of Buddhism in India was not the end of the story by any means. Buddhist teachings and practices had already been transmitted far beyond the confines of the subcontinent to places where, coming in contact with new influences and circumstances, they were in time to undergo further revitalizing phases of development. We can trace three principal transmissions.

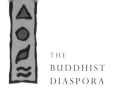

1: THE SOUTHERN TRANSMISSION

Though the Mahayana and Vajrayana were both introduced many centuries ago, the brand of Buddhism that nowadays predominates in South-east Asia is the Theravada, literally the 'Way of the Elders', which can trace its origins back to the seminal pre-Mahayana school of Buddhism.

Sri Lanka

The first successful Buddhist missionary effort was Sri Lanka, and Theravada Buddhism was brought to this gem-like tropical island in the third century CE.

Mahayana and Tantric Buddhism later arrived in Sri Lanka, and their devotees came into contention with those of the orthodox Theravada. However, the matter was settled by a council in 1160, which suppressed all non-Theravada schools. Later, Sri Lanka suffered political upheaval due to European colonization and invasion from south India, and by the mid-eighteenth century its Buddhism was in such a parlous state that bhikshus (monks) had to be imported from elsewhere to maintain the tradition. Revival got under way during the latter part of the nineteenth century, however, generated both by local Buddhists and by European sympathizers, such as the pioneer Theosophists H S Olcott and H P Blavatsky. A relatively healthy, if rather conservative tradition, with a scholarly bias, currently survives in strife-torn Sri Lanka, but there is also a forest tradition of secluded meditator monks and nuns.

Burma

Various forms of Buddhism were also introduced into Burma (Myanmar) and, between the eleventh and thirteenth centuries CE, a wonderful Buddhist culture bloomed at Pagan. Because of various schisms and dissensions, however, a 'canonically valid monastic succession' was introduced from Sri Lanka in the fifteenth century, since when Sri Lankan Theravada has been the predominant tradition. During the British occupation (1885–1948), Buddhism became closely associated with Burmese nationalism.

Thailand

Sri Lankan Theravada was established as the predominant tradition in Thailand in the fourteenth century CE. Today Thai Buddhism is highly hierarchic and organized. It also comes under a degree of state supervision and the king is the Supreme Patriarch. Not surprisingly, therefore, the local 'church' has its radicals and reformers as well as its unbending conservatives. Much of its vitality, however, lies away from the towns and cities in rural forest areas where serious practitioners ordain and get down to the real business of doing Buddhism. One well-known modern master of the forest tradition is Ajahn Chah, who has trained many Western monks, notably Ajahn Sumedho, the American founder of four new Theravada monasteries in Britain and others elsewhere.

Laos and Kampuchea

Thai influence has also been responsible for the predominance of Sri Lankan Theravada in Laos and Kampuchea. Tragically, traumatic political strife decimated the Buddhist traditions of both countries. In Laos, a small remnant of the Sangha is trying to re-establish itself. In Kampuchea, the position is highly uncertain.

Indonesia

Indonesia boasts the largest Buddhist monument in South-east Asia: the massive stupa-temple of Borobodur on Java. There is also other evidence that various forms of Buddhism were transmitted to the region in the past but were eclipsed by the coming of Islam in the fifteenth century. Today, however, modest efforts are being made to revive both Theravada and Mahayana Buddhism there.

ABOVE *H S Olcott, who, along with Madame Blavatsky, helped to revive the Buddhist tradition in Sri Lanka during the late nineteenth century.*

ABOVE *Madame Blavatsky, founder of the Theosophist Society, along with two of her colleagues.*

2: THE NORTHERN TRANSMISSION

The Northern Transmission was constellated and launched from a region that we might call the North West Springboard. It comprised parts of north-west India and modern Pakistan, Afghanistan, Central Asia and Chinese Sinkiang. This was once a dynamic region through which great trade and migration routes passed, many cultures met and many people settled.

States such as Gandhara, situated in the North-west Frontier Region, with Purushapura (modern Peshawar) as its capital, became immortalized in Buddhist myth and legend as places where the Dharma once flourished gloriously. Sadly, all this had been largely swept away by the seventh century CE.

China

Buddhism reached China in the first century CE from the North West Springboard, carried along the Silk Route by merchants, travellers and Buddhist monks. Small Buddhist groups emerged among expatriate communities in the capital, Loyang, and other cities, and texts began to be translated. The Chinese themselves were apparently resistant to Buddhism at first because their own Confucian tradition preached very different notions, but they were brought around during the Period of Disunity that followed the fall of the Later Han Dynasty. Buddhism, with its teachings on anitya (impermanence) and duhkha (suffering), no doubt offered consolations that the intellectual and aristocratic élite were not able to find in their native traditions during this turbulent and insecure period.

During the Period of Disunity (220–589), Buddhism became actively patronized and encouraged by the foreign dynasties that established themselves in the north; it also found favour in the courts of Han Chinese rulers in the south. Royal blessing and the

LEFT *The ruins of the Silk Route city of Gaochang in China. Buddhism was carried to China in the first century CE by monks and merchants who travelled along the Silk Route.*

support of the literati ensured its success.
Soon enormous numbers of Chinese were
ordained as monks and nuns – by around
514 CE there were two million of them –
marvellous monasteries and temples were
built, and the work of translating the
scriptures into Chinese was undertaken with
great industry. Special 'translation teams'
were set up, often headed by a master such as
the great Kumarajiva, who was brought to
China as one of the spoils of war. Popular
forms of Buddhism also percolated down to
the ordinary folk, who never became
exclusively Buddhist but practised the religion
alongside the indigenous traditions of Taoism,
Confucianism and the folk cults.

Buddhism in China reached its apogee
during the Sui and T'ang Dynasties
(581–907 CE). The work of importation and
assimilation done, a fully Sinicized Buddhism
then emerged, forged by the creative
interaction of the Indian teachings with local
traditions, notably Taoism, and by the Chinese
genius itself.

The success of Buddhism had caused
backlash before, but in 845 the 'church',
which now had riches and power enough to
eclipse those of the straitened emperor
himself, was subjected to a draconian blow
from which it never fully recovered.
Buddhism was not actually outlawed, but
monks and nuns were required to go back to
lay life, monasteries and temples were closed,
and monastic lands, slaves and treasuries were
seized. The Ch'an (Zen) and Pure Land
schools were resilient enough to survive this
holocaust, but thereafter Chinese Buddhism
went into an almost fatal decline. True, a
thousand years later, in the early part of the
present century, efforts were made to
regenerate it, often with the help of Western
sympathizers, but the Communist Revolution
in 1948, and even more so the Cultural
Revolution of 1966–76, dealt further savage
blows to the already ailing remnant of this
once glorious tradition. In the more relaxed
climate of the 1980s, Buddhism was accorded
a degree of tolerance, monasteries began to
function again and people took the robe,
though not in large numbers.

Korea

China formerly dominated Korea and much of
the region comprising modern Vietnam, so
Chinese forms of Buddhism were transmitted
there. Korean Zen has experienced something
of a revival in modern times, but this follows
on the heels of some 600 years of decline.

BELOW *Karakoram,
China, an area that was
once part of the Silk
Route. The nomadic
people of this region still
practise Buddhism.*

RIGHT *The Japanese*
samurai class were
attracted to the Zen
philosophy. As a result,
the austere samurai
values and practices
infiltrated Zen
monasteries.

Japan

Starting in the sixth century CE, Japan also
received the Buddha-dharma, primarily from
China. Here again royal favour initially
ensured success, the local rulers believing that
Buddhism possessed special magical powers
that could be invoked to protect both state
and dynasty. Buddhism also had to come to
terms with the indigenous Shinto cult, whose
priesthood initially put up a vigorous
resistance. An accommodation between
Shinto and Buddhism was, however,
successfully forged and lasted down to 1868.

The golden age of Japanese Buddhism
was the turbulent Kamakura Period
(1185–1333 CE), when the samurai class
seized power from the decadent imperial
aristocracy and established the Shogunate or
military government at Kamakura. The
samurai, who were professional fighters,
found the teachings of the anti-philosophical,
no-nonsense Zen school suited their needs

admirably and adopted it with vigour. Sumurai
values and training methods also reciprocally
infiltrated Zen monasteries, particularly those
of the Rinzai (Lin-chi) school.

After this fruitful period, Japanese
Buddhism lost its creative vigour and a phase
of decline set in. Matters were not helped by
the fact that important Buddhist centres
were broken for political reasons, and the
religion was brought under the stifling hand
of state control. The Zen tradition again
survived best. With the Meiji Restoration
(1868), when imperial rule was restored
following the demise of the Tokugawa
Shogunate, there was another anti-Buddhist
backlash, caused by an upsurge of nationalism
and a Shinto revival. But Buddhism was by
now strongly rooted enough not merely to
weather the storm but to be galvanized into
something of a revival. In modern times,
following the trauma of Japan's defeat in the
Second World War, the lay-oriented Nichiren
sects have attracted mass followings.

Tibet

Despite attempts to introduce Chinese Zen Buddhism into Tibet, the Tibetans oriented themselves to Indian Buddhism. In particular the magic and mystery of Tantric Vajrayana appealed to the national temperament, resonating and fruitfully interacting with the indigenous traditions of Bön (originally a death cult) and the animistic folk religions.

We can trace two principal transmissions of Buddhism to Tibet: an initial one begun during the seventh century CE, and a second one starting around the year 1000. During the first phase (c640–838 CE), both monastic and Tantric Buddhism were introduced. A beginning was also made on translating Buddhist texts into Tibetan. During the second phase (c1000–1959), a number of Sarma or 'New' schools established themselves, most of them of the cleaned-up Tantric variety, in which non-Tantric or 'Sutra' elements were integrated with Tantric ones.

We cannot fairly talk of a Tibetan transformation of Buddhism as we can of a

Chinese one. To the Tibetans, India was a kind of holy land and the Buddhist teachings from there were sacrosanct. After Indian Buddhism had been wiped out, the Tibetans saw themselves as custodians of those hallowed traditions. Yet it cannot be denied that up on the heights of the Tibetan plateau, effectively cut off from the outside world by formidable geographical barriers, their 1,000-year custodianship imbued Vajrayana Buddhism with a new tone and colour. That this was preserved almost intact until the middle of the present century was a kind of miracle, which makes the Chinese decimation of Tibetan Buddhism during the Cultural Revolution (1966–76) all the more poignant.

The Tibetan style of Buddhism spread into Mongolia, parts of China and even into Russia, where it was established among the Buryat people, who before collectivization grazed their herds and flocks to the east of Lake Baikal in eastern Siberia, and the Kalmucks; they carried it in their migration from Asia to the Lower Volga region. It also reached the Himalayan kingdoms of Bhutan, Sikkim, Nepal and Ladakh. No momentous new developments emerged in these areas.

ABOVE *Tibetan monks at a religious festivity.*

LEFT *A Bhutanese dancer. Tibetan Buddhism, with all its colourful rituals, spread to surrounding areas, such as Bhutan.*

3: THE WESTERN TRANSMISSION

Buddhist teachings reached the West back in the midst of antiquity, so legend tells us, but significant and lasting connections in Europe were not forged until the nineteenth century. Ironically, imperialism was a powerful indirect cause. European administrators, scholars and missionaries working in Oriental colonies began to take an interest in the lost or declining Buddhist traditions, to investigate sites archaeologically and, having mastered the intricacies of Sanskrit, Pali, Chinese and other languages, to translate texts and study their contents. Only then did the Western world – and the Eastern world – become fully aware of the panoramic grandeur of Buddhism.

At the same time, the failure of Western religion to provide real spiritual nourishment, and the growing disillusionment with science and materialistic values, caused many to begin to explore the Eastern religions. Brave new movements emerged, among them Theosophy, an ambitious syncretism devised by a formidable Russian lady named Helena Petrovna Blavatsky. The canons of Theosophy proclaim that the great religions of the world are eroded remnants of a great 'wisdom religion' that once existed and to which Buddhism most closely approximates. Whether they accurately understood Buddhism or not is a moot point, but the early Theosophists usefully commended it to the attention of the Western public, did sterling work in helping to revive the religion in Sri Lanka and elsewhere, and paved the way for the modern Western resurgence.

During the early twentieth century, European Buddhists gradually began to disentangle themselves from Theosophy and started to study the teachings with a view to putting them into practice. Journals went into print, and a few intrepid pioneers took ordination. The trauma of the First World War increased interest, and during the interwar period new societies began to flourish, missionaries from the East arrived and effective propagandists emerged.

RIGHT *The Buddha by the French artist Odilon Redon (1840–1916).*

Buddhism reached both the east and the west coasts of the United States during the nineteenth century. On the east coast it attracted the attention of New England intellectuals such as H D Thoreau and Ralph Waldo Emerson, while on the west coast Ch'an and Pure Land Buddhism were part of the baggage of the Chinese immigrants who came to work in railway construction or in gold prospecting. Later Japanese immigrants brought their own traditions too. An important milestone was the World Parliament of Religions convened in Chicago in 1893. This brought the Zen master Soyen Shaku to the United States, and led to his pupil, D T Suzuki, spending a number of years working in the USA.

During the 1960s, in many Western countries, enormous numbers of people from

all walks of life began to gravitate to Buddhism, particularly young people who were both disaffected with conventional materialistic values and affluent enough to be able to explore and experiment with alternatives. With the diaspora of lamas after the Chinese takeover of Tibet in 1959, moreover, there was at last access to Tibetan Buddhist teachings, whereas before, Theravada and Zen had been most available and hence most popular. There was also a new commitment to practice, especially to meditation, and, by the early 1980s, Theravada bhikshus (monks) were taking the robe on Western soil.

There has been much high-quality Buddhist scholarship in the West, and an enormous number of texts have been published in translation, particularly in English.

Contemporary Western trends and issues

WOMEN

Traditionally in Oriental society women are accorded a very subservient rôle and this tendency has fully infiltrated Buddhism. In all Vinaya-based traditions, for instance, a Buddhist nun of many years standing is deemed inferior to a monk ordained for just a few hours. Some Oriental traditions, moreover, transmit the notion that it is difficult if not impossible for women to become Enlightened; the best they can do is accrue sufficient merit in this lifetime to qualify for a future male rebirth. In the present climate of sexual equality such out-moded attitudes raise considerable difficulties.

SOCIAL ACTION

Traditionally Buddhists have been socially and politically quiescent – or acquiescent, prepared often to coexist with ruthless régimes. Indeed, until very recently Western concepts such as democracy, justice and freedom of expression were largely unknown in the East, where feudal forms of political life predominated. Following this tradition, 'politics' has tended to be regarded as a dirty word in some Western Buddhist circles, as though anything smacking even slightly of it will contaminate the pristine purity of the Dharma. Many Western Buddhists, on the other hand, feel it impossible to turn their backs on such issues as repression, economic exploitation, racism, militarism, environmental destruction and genocide. They have found much inspiration in the life and teachings of the expatriate Vietnamese monk Thich Nhat Hanh, originator of the term 'Engaged Buddhism', who is now based at Plum Village in France, where he works to alleviate the suffering of his people and generally to promote the cause of peace. Of course, modern Buddhist social activists would want to avoid the old confrontational style of political engagement, with its us-and-them psychology that all too easily leads to bitter and destructive controversy. But equally they are not prepared to sit on their meditation cushions, working out their own salvation, however diligently, while the rest of the world suffers.

INDIVIDUALISM

Traditional Buddhist schools, because they developed in feudal situations, tended to be based on feudal models. For example, in Japanese Rinzai Zen the teacher–pupil relationship echoes that of the samurai clan boss and his subservient retainers. There was little scope in such contexts for concepts such as independence of thought and action; the individual was a passive unit in a collectivity directed from above. Modern Westerners can conform to such situations only by performing psychological contortions or else by regressing to a kind of adolescent parent–child stance and thereby avoiding adult responsibility. Real and positive development, therefore, demands that the mature ego be given a place in today's Western Buddhism.

WISDOM 1
THE BASIC TEACHINGS

*W*isdom is, in a sense, both the beginning of the path and the
end, where it assumes an altogether higher or transcendent form.
The wisdom that lies at the beginning is a grasp of the Buddha's basic
teachings. These are not rigid articles of faith that we have to embrace totally.
The Buddha recognized that truth cannot be pinned down once and for all.
What held good last week or year is superseded in the changed conditions of
today. 'Can you nail down the clouds in the sky, or tie them up with rope?'
asks the Zen master. So, in the free spirit of the Kalama Sutra, the Buddha's
teachings should be regarded as skilful means (upaya) for obtaining
certain results. We are invited to experiment with them to see
if they work for us, in the context of our own everyday lives.

DUHKHA: 'SUFFERING'

It was the problem of duhkha, rather than abstract questions like 'Who made the world?' and 'What happens to us after death?', that shocked the Buddha into his own spiritual quest. Duhkha is often translated as 'suffering' but, in fact, it covers a whole spectrum of psycho-emotional states, from a mild sense that things are not quite right to intense physical and mental pain. It may also be taken to mean that there is no lasting peace or rest in life; that we are forever under pressure and subject to disruption. This should not be taken to mean, however, that Buddhists believe that life is *all* suffering – a common misconception. The opposite of duhkha, sukha – pleasant feeling – is fully admitted. But pleasure and its ancillaries present us with few problems. Duhkha is problematic, however – and that is why we need to do something about it.

The person that desires to have *only* pleasures and refuses pain expends an enormous amount of energy resisting life – and at the same time misses out enormously. He or she is on a self-defeating mission in any case, for just as we evade certain forms of suffering we inevitably fall victim to others. Underlying our glitzy modern consumer culture there is a deep spiritual undernourishment and malaise that manifests all kinds of symptoms: nervous disorders, loneliness, alienation, purposelessness …

So blanking out or running away will take us nowhere. If we really want to solve our problems – and the world's problems, for they stem from the same roots – we must open up and accept the reality of suffering with full awareness, as it strikes us, physically, emotionally, mentally, spiritually, in the here-now. Then, strange as it may seem, we reap vast rewards. For suffering has its positive side. From it we derive the experience of *depth*: of the fullness of our humanity. This puts us fully in touch with other people and the rest of the Universe. Suffering can also bring out the full grandeur of our race, its heroic and best potential.

The great American writer Henry Miller wrote:

❧

Only in sorrow and suffering does man draw close to his fellow man; only then, it seems, does his life become beautiful.[1]

❧

If, therefore, we want to live as wholly human beings, we must be prepared to follow the old heroes willingly and consciously into the dark labyrinths and confront the grim denizens that lurk there. All we have to fear is our fear. All we need for protection is courage – and a little wise guidance.

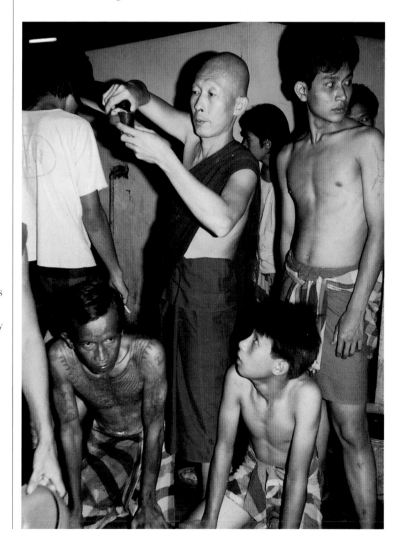

DELUSION
AND 'NOT-SELF'

A primary cause of suffering is delusion: our inability, because of a subtly wilful blindness, to see things the way they truly are but instead in a distorted way. The world is in fact a seamless and dynamic unity: a single living organism that is constantly undergoing change. Our minds, however, chop it up into separate, static bits and pieces, which we then try mentally and physically to manipulate.

One of the mind's most dear creations is the idea of the person – and, closest to home, of a very special person that each one of us calls 'I': a separate, enduring ego or self. In a moment, then, the seamless universe is cut in two. There is 'I' – and there is all the rest. That means conflict – and pain, for 'I' cannot control that fathomless vastness against which it is set. It will try, of course, as a flea might pit itself against an elephant, but it is a vain enterprise.

Central to the Buddha's teaching is the doctrine of anatman: 'not-self'. This does not deny that the notion of an 'I' works in the everyday world. In fact, we need a solid, stable ego to function in society. However, 'I' is not real in an ultimate sense. It is a 'name': a fictional construct that bears no correspondence to what is really the case. Because of this disjunction all kinds of problems ensue.

Once our minds have constructed the notion of 'I', it becomes our central reference point. We attach to it and identify with it totally. We attempt to advance what appears to be its interests, to defend it against real or apparent threats and menaces. And we look for ego-affirmation at every turn: confirmation that we exist and are valued. The Gordian Knot of preoccupations arising from all this absorbs us exclusively, at times to the point of obsession. This is, however, a narrow and constricted way of being. Though we cannot see it when caught in the convolutions of ego, there is something in us that is larger and deeper: a wholly other way of being.

RIGHT Prince Siddhartha sees the four omens – an old man, a sick man, a corpse and a monk. This, his first encounter with the four elements of life, sets him on his quest to discover how to deal with life's pain and suffering.

SKANDHAS:
'Components of the Individual'

If the idea of 'I' is a fiction, we may justifiably ask how it arises in the first place. The classic Buddhist answer would run along these lines:

If we take a motor car, for instance, we feel quite sure about what we have ... until we start taking it apart. Once we have removed the bodywork, stripped down the engine, taken out the gearbox, removed the wheels and so on – what's left? We don't have a car any more, just a set of spare parts.

It is the same with a person. That too can be stripped down to its basic components, which are traditionally divided into five standard categories: the so-called skandhas or 'groups'.

There is 1 the category of the physical, which includes the body and its five senses; 2 that of feeling; 3 perception; 4 mental formations (impulses and emotions); and 5 consciousness or mind. When these groups of components come together in proper working order, the right conditions exist for the illusion of a self and a person to arise. But once they break down and go their separate ways — as at physical death, for instance — then that self or person cannot be found.

What remains is not nothingness, annihilation, however. The Buddha defined that as a wrong view. Nor is it some sort of eternal *something* — another wrong view. There is an elusive 'middle way' transcending both annihilationism and eternalism — in fact all dualities, including life and death. We must seek the truth here.

DHARMAS:
'Ultimate Elements'

In the Abhidharma, the philosophical systematizations of the early Buddhist schools, the search for the ultimate elements of the world-process is taken as far as it will go on the micro level. These ultimate elements are called 'dharmas' — in the Sarvastivadin system there are 75 dharmas in all — and are said to be insubstantial appearances, in the words of T Stcherbatsky, 'momentary flashings into the phenomenal world out of an unknown source'. Perpetually in a state of agitation until finally calmed in Nirvana, they are forces rather than substances.

True reality, then, is the dance of these mysterious, evanescent dharmas as they cluster into groups and flow in what appear to be streams (santana). The deluded mind, however, discerns 'things' and 'personalities' here, just as a person looking up into the sky may see the shapes of faces or maps or trees where in fact there are just configurations of cloud; or a thirsty person in a desert may see a lake of cool water, which is in fact only a mirage.

The teaching on dharmas — as indeed all the other of the Buddha's teachings — is not meant to be accepted on trust. It can only be understood through meditation and practice. The dedicated practitioner should actually be able to make his mind so calm, clear and still that he can actually see these infinitesimal 'flashings' — these dharmas — of which there are many to the split second. In this way he will once and for all see through the shadow play world of conventional existence and never again be its dupe. Needless to say, of course, only a very gifted meditator practising in ideal circumstances for many years will be able to reach this kind of virtuoso level.

ABOVE *A Sri Lankan monk meditating in the lotus position.*

Dependent Origination

A popular explanation of the way causation works in the cycles of life and death is set out in the teachings of Dependent Origination (Pratitya Samutpada). We have already seen how the Buddha rejected the notion of a Creator God or Prime Mover. All phenomena in the Universe are produced within the cosmos by internal causes. That is to say, each phenomenon is the cause of a further phenomenon, which in its turn will go on to be a cause of ... and so on, ad infinitum.

But let us take a loose example. A young man sees a shiny sports car. It inspires strong feelings in him – he imagines the elation as he drives down the road at 100mph, with the hood down, the wind streaming through his hair, a pretty girl beside him. Desire is born: he wants to possess the car. So he borrows the money to buy it. Once he has it, his life changes. He has to work harder in order to run and maintain the car – and to pay back his debt. It is a struggle, but he is so attached to the car that he cannot bear the idea of losing it. Things get difficult, so he takes on extra work. Gradually stress and overwork undermine his health. He falls ill with a kidney complaint. A few years later he dies, which in due course occasions a new birth. All this happened, the Buddhist explanation would run, because he was deluded: he thought that true fulfilment lay in getting that sports car, whereas in fact doing so merely led to a series of escalating complications. The rebirth resulting from his death will merely repeat a similar process ... until the lesson is learnt and a firm resolution arises to seek escape from the endless cycles of old mistakes.

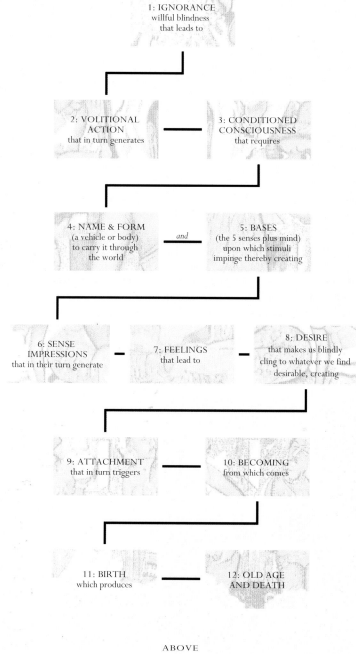

1: IGNORANCE
willful blindness
that leads to

2: VOLITIONAL
ACTION
that in turn generates

3: CONDITIONED
CONSCIOUSNESS
that requires

4: NAME & FORM
(a vehicle or body)
to carry it through
the world

and

5: BASES
(the 5 senses plus mind)
upon which stimuli
impinge thereby creating

6: SENSE
IMPRESSIONS
that in their turn generate

7: FEELINGS
that lead to

8: DESIRE
that makes us blindly
cling to whatever we find
desirable, creating

9: ATTACHMENT
that in turn triggers

10: BECOMING
from which comes

11: BIRTH
which produces

12: OLD AGE
AND DEATH

ABOVE
Chart showing the 12 links (nidana)
within the human life span.

KARMA: 'Consequences'

What force joins each link in the chain of Dependent Origination, keeping the Wheel of Life in perpetual spin? The answer is karma. The word – karman is in fact the correct Sanskrit form – has now penetrated the Western consciousness, though, from the Buddhist point of view at least, in somewhat distorted guise. It is often called the Law of Cause and Effect, so it is about the consequences of actions of body, speech and mind. And consequences are very important in Buddhism.

Any action that is willed, however subtly, by the person who performs it will always produce a future 'ripening' and ultimately a 'fruit' of similar moral quality, because in the human sphere karma operates in an ethical manner. So an unethical action will induce a comeback of like kind in this life or some future rebirth; and the same goes for morally good or indifferent actions that are willed and freely undertaken. In the Bible it says something similar: that we reap what we sow. If we want to progress spiritually – or even just to live with minimum aggravation – it

therefore behoves us to be very careful how we speak and act, for there is no way we can escape the consequences. As it says in the *Dhammapada*, a concise and poetic early Buddhist text:

∞

If a man speaks or acts with an impure mind, pain pursues him, even as the wheel follows the ox that draws the cart.[2]

∞

This teaching should not be used as a pretext for unkind judgementalism, however. For instance, were someone to fall ill, a censorious person might declare, 'Ah well, that's the result of past karma. He's merely reaping what he sowed.' This, however, is to ignore the fact that non-karmic forces are also in play. Our bodies, being organic, are subject to growth and decay regardless of how we behave. Various circumstantial factors also have a bearing on how things turn out. In any case, who is it that performs an action? If ego is ultimately an illusion, there is no doer, just the deed. Where then does moral responsibility lie?

LEFT *The temptation of the Buddha. As the Buddha sat under the bodhi tree he was visited by earthly temptations, but by remaining detached yet alert he was able to neutralize their power over him.*

∞

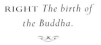

REBIRTH AND DEATH

As must have become quite clear by now, Buddhism does not hold with nihilistic views of death. There is no yawning abyss of pure nothingness into which we finally disappear. There is just Samsara, the cyclic world-process – and escape from it.

Buddhists are often thought to subscribe to the idea of reincarnation. This is not strictly true. Reincarnation presupposes that some kind of enduring soul or essence, something with unchanging personal imprints, commutes from body to body down through the marches of time. As we have seen, however, the Buddha denied the existence of any soul that might reincarnate. What he did admit of was something slightly different, which we might call *rebirth*. This maintains

that there is a *causal connection* between one life and a subsequent one. Nothing is handed on in the transaction, however; the following life is a completely new one. But the form it takes is conditioned by the previous one. It is rather like a billiard ball flying across the green baize of a billiard table. It hits another ball and that cannons on at a speed and in a direction that owes something to the first ball (and also to other incidental factors), but it does not take away anything material or essential from the first ball.

Strictly speaking, we die and are reborn from moment to moment. If one were to look at two photographs of the same person, taken 20 or 30 years apart, would one see the same person, the same face and body, the same look

RIGHT *The birth of the Buddha.*

in the eyes? Or would all those things be
different? The answer is self-evident. Physical
death, however, is undeniably a more obvious
and disturbing 'death' than the smaller ones
that happen from moment to moment.

The odds in favour of a human rebirth, from
where alone escape from Samsara is possible,
are said to be very slender. If a blind turtle
swimming in a vast ocean came up for air once
every one hundred years, what would be the
likelihood of it putting its head through a
golden yoke floating on the surface? So, if we
are favoured with a 'precious human rebirth',
we should take care to put it to good use in
the interests of achieving liberation, otherwise
we may be dispatched to the other grim
'destinations' – the hell realms, the realm of
the hungry ghosts and so forth – and
circulated there for aeons before we get
another chance.

The bardo

In Tibetan Buddhism we find a detailed
analysis of the states that arise in the 'bardo'
or intermediate state that intervenes
between one life and another. The bardo is a
terrifying phantasmagoria in which all kinds
of spectres, gods, demons and other
apparitions loom up before the bewildered
disembodied consciousness[3] traversing it.
Wonderful 'luminosities' appear too, but
the consciousness traversing the bardo will
usually be too confused to see them for
what they are and will instead be swept
onwards towards rebirth, which will take
place within a maximum period of 49 days.

LEFT *The death of
the Buddha. His
disciples gathered round
where he finally lay in a
grove of sala trees in
Kushinagara, not far
from his birth-place
at Lumbini.*

CHANGE AND IMPERMANENCE

The Buddha stressed the dynamic nature of existence. This resonates with the ideas of some early Greek philosophers, such as Heraclitus, who maintained that 'All is flux' and 'You can't step into the same river twice.'

In order to live skilfully, in harmony with the dynamic Universe, it is essential to accept the reality of change and impermanence. The wise person therefore travels lightly, with a minimum of clutter, maintaining the proverbial 'open mind' in all situations, for he or she knows that tomorrow's reality will not be the same as today's. He or she will also have learnt the divine art of letting go – which means not being attached to people and possessions and situations, but rather, when the time for parting comes, allowing that to happen graciously.

BELOW A detail from the Wheel of Life. At the hub of the wheel is desire, aversion and delusion represented by a cock, snake and pig, all chasing each other in an unbreakable circular chain.

DESIRE

If the basic project of mainstream Buddhist practice is to unmask the ego illusion for what it is, one of the main prongs of attack is directed against desire. Desire gets a very bad press in the Buddhist scriptures. It is a poison, a disease, a madness. There is no living in a body that is subject to desire, for it is like a blazing house.

Now, desire lives and grows by being indulged. When not indulged by the application of ethical restraint and awareness, on the other hand, it stabilizes and begins to diminish, though this is not an easy or comfortable process, for the old urges clamour for satisfaction for a long time.

This kind of practice, of course, cuts directly against the main currents of modern consumer society, where desire is energetically encouraged and refined to new pitches and variations by the powerful agencies of marketing and publicity. But it also cuts against the more moderate desires – for family, wealth, sense-pleasure and so on – sanctioned in simpler, more traditional societies, including the one into which the Buddha was born. We can never be at peace while desire is nagging at us.

The flip-side of desire is aversion, a pushing away of that which we dislike as opposed to a grasping on to things we like. Aversion too must be put to rest.

Desire, aversion and their bedfellow, delusion, are the basic faults of frailties of character that drive us through the painful cycles of Samsara. They are symbolically represented at the very hub of the Wheel of Life by a cock, snake and pig, all chasing each other and biting each others' tails in an unbreakable circular chain.

HIGHER QUALITIES AND VIRTUES

Through taking the medicine that the wise doctor, the Buddha, prescribes – that is, through regular, balanced practice, usually over a fairly extensive period of time – many of the complicated problems that arise in life sort themselves out quite organically. Time and energy are at the same time freed for actively inculcating moral qualities such as patience, kindness, resolution, sympathetic joy for the successes of others, compassion for their suffering, and so forth. There is also more latitude for study and meditation.

As practice deepens over time, more specialized qualities will arise, including the higher form of wisdom we mentioned earlier. This enables the practitioner to see things as they really are, clearly, no longer through the distorting lenses of desire-based fantasy, projection and so forth.

As the process proceeds towards its culmination, detachment from both the world and the self advances. The urges within die away until finally the practitioner is capable of such dispassionate acceptance of all the vicissitudes of life that even death ceases to frighten him.

NIRVANA: *'Release'*

The end of the path is likened in the early
scriptures to the blowing out of a candle
when there ceases to be fuel to keep it alight.
This is Nirvana. Identification with a self has
ceased; indeed all urge to exist as a person –
or to exist at all – has ceased. Desire and
aversion have been pacified. Delusion has been
replaced by clarity. At the micro level, the
agitation of the dharmas has completely
calmed down. Cyclic existence, birth and
death, are transcended.

We must be careful not to reify this as sheer
nothingness – or as a super transcendental
something. It is beyond birth and death,
existence and non-existence – and utterly
beyond the power of the mind to know or of
words to tell. We are assured, however, that it
is the greatest bliss. Life in the body may still
continue, and teaching may take place too – as
in the case of the Buddha – but, ultimately,
there is a further and equally ineffable
transition at physical death. This is
Parinirvana. Of the Buddha's own final passing
or Parinirvana, it is written:

*As a flame blown out by the wind
Goes to rest and cannot be defined,
So the wise man freed from individuality
Goes to rest and cannot be defined.
Gone beyond all images –
Gone beyond the power of words.*[4]

ABOVE *The Parinirvana of the Buddha. After the
death of the physical body, the Buddha then passed
into Parinirvana – the further transition of the
Enlightened one who has reached Nirvana.*

ABOVE LEFT *Buddha seated upon a lotus throne
beneath the bo tree, surrounded by scenes from his life.*

WISDOM 2
MAHAYANA DEVELOPMENTS

The Buddha said that all things were subject to change; therefore, it was quite consistent with basic principles that later generations of Buddhists should modify, restate and develop his teachings.

This chapter looks at the most important developments that took place after the rise of the Mahayana, in particular the reformulations of the anatman teaching, which many regard as the key teaching that distinguishes Buddhism from other Indian religious systems.

The anatman teaching was originally very much a reaction against the notion of atman, which is quite central to mainstream brahmanical religion. There is, so brahmins and rishis believe, an Ultimate Reality or Self that they call Brahman, which can be found, not in some heavenly sphere, but in the human heart, in which case it is called atman or the self. Actually there is no difference between Brahman and atman. The Self and the self are one.

The great rishis and yogis of the *Upanishads* stressed the unknowable nature of Brahman/atman. The best that they could do was to describe it in negative terms: *Neti, neti* ('Not this, not this'). The problem is, of course, that the thinking mind cannot let things rest. It will always conspire to trap them in the net of thought and describe them through the medium of words – even when warned not to do so. So gradually the idea of atman began to degenerate. Images and ideas and verbiage were projected onto the blank screen of that great mystery – until it was a mystery no more.

The Buddha's mission was therefore essentially a reformist one. He wanted to purify the notion of atman of all those projections and restore its unknowableness. So, when he taught anatman, he was not asserting that there is no atman, no self (and hence no Self – no Ultimate Reality), as indeed many Buddhists have thought. *Rather he meant that anything you think or say about atman is not atman.* Atman is beyond all words and ideas. Therefore, you cannot grasp it with the thinking mind. But perhaps you can purify and open yourself in order that it can fill you. Then you can *be* it.

Even the Buddha's formulation of the anatman doctrine, then, insofar as it is itself verbal-conceptual, cannot be perfect or definitive. Not surprisingly, therefore, not long after his death, during the period when the eighteen pre-Mahayana schools flourished in India, slight distortions of the teaching began to creep in. It had probably begun to lose vitality too. With the rise of the Mahayana, therefore, new attempts were made to revitalize and restore the teaching to its original purity. In the process, as we shall see, the whole thing goes through a 180-degree shift, from negative formulations to more positive ones.

LEFT *The Buddha
teaching.*

SHUNYATA: *'Emptiness'*

With the rise of the Mahayana, we find the anatman teaching reformulated in the concept of Shunyata ('Emptiness')[1]. This Emptiness is not pure nothingness, of course; nor is it a kind of transcendental something. Rather it is a medicine to remedy the compulsive illusion-making habits of our minds, particularly their tendency to think of persons and things as separate, self-created and self-sustaining.

Shunyata indicates, therefore, not the presence of something but rather a resounding lack or void, specifically a lack of inherent existence or 'own nature' (svabhava). This goes as much for dharmas, those ultimate essences of the world-process, as it does for people and things. In the Mahayana, dharmas are decreed unequivocally to be empty, along with everything else. Even Emptiness is ultimately empty!

OPPOSITE *Tibetan
monks outside their
temple. Over the years,
the Buddha's teachings
were adapted to suit the
different situations and
temperaments of its
adherents in different
parts of the world.*

The bodhisattva and compassion

As well as dissipating delusion, an understanding of Shunyata is said to produce a deep compassion (karuna) for the suffering of sentient beings. Compassion means 'to suffer with' – actually to share and feel the sufferings of others as though they are one's own. Obviously a breaking-down of those psychological boundaries that divided 'I' from others has taken place here. In Mahayana teaching, compassion is thought to lead to a deep resolve to fulfil the goals of the spiritual life in order to help others to become free – particularly free from suffering. This is technically called bodhicitta ('Enlightenment mind') and its presence elevates a person to the status of a bodhisattva ('Enlightenment being').

To become a bodhisattva one must already be well advanced along the path. One must have fully understood the Buddha's teachings on karma and rebirth, Dependent Origination and so forth, had insight into Emptiness and felt the stirrings of deep compassion. In some Buddhist texts, it is stated that some advanced bodhisattvas have actually attained Enlightenment; that is, they are buddhas, no less. In others, however, it is suggested that they 'postpone' their own Enlightenment. Mostly, however, the term is clearly meant to signify someone who is a buddha-in-the-making, motivated altruistically rather than selfishly.

A fine impression of what it practically means to try to live the bodhisattva life is given by the Indian teacher Shantideva in his classic poem *Bodhisattvacharyavatara* ('Guide to the Bodhisattva's Way of Life')[2]. Shantideva determines to follow

ABOVE *While sitting meditating beneath a tree, the Buddha was visited by Sujata, who presented him with a bowl and a golden cup of water. When the Buddha saw the golden cup float upstream, he recognized it as a sign that he would soon gain Enlightenment.*

ABOVE *A Tibetan painting showing Amitabha, the Buddha of Infinite Light, in his Western Paradise of Sukhavati. Above on the left is the Shakyamuni Buddha and on the right is the second Buddha Akshobya. Below are various bodhisattvas.*

the way of the bodhisattva and be the doctor, medicine and nurse 'for all sick beings in the world until everyone is healed'. Repenting wholeheartedly of all his former sins, he determines to bind the 'crazy elephant' of the mind. He will therefore examine his mind before doing or saying anything and, if he finds his motivation tainted, will 'remain like a piece of wood'.

He will also be open and at times 'be the pupil of everyone' – excellent advice! Conscious too that one moment of anger can destroy the good generated by wholesome deeds performed 'over a thousand aeons', he will practise patience. If someone hurts him, he will reflect that this is just the ripening of his own past karma, and bear no malice. He will also restrain his sexual passions.

The bodhisattva will consciously develop enthusiasm to counter any disposition to laziness that might impair his practice. Then, 'by seeing the equality of self and others' he will give up all 'self-cherishing' and 'practise that holy secret: the exchanging of self for others'. He will actually conceive of others as 'I', as his own self, their bodies as his body, and take to himself their suffering.

Finally, in true bodhisattva style, Shantideva dedicates all merit (good karma) that might accrue to him to the liberation of all beings everywhere, and hopes that they will 'obtain an ocean of happiness and joy'. For the true bodhisattva's compassion is never limited to a few chosen beneficiaries. It goes out equally to the whole world, like the warmth of the sun.

PRAJÑAPARAMITA:
'Perfection of Wisdom'

The first major Mahayana teaching to emerge was the Prajñaparamita or 'Perfection of Wisdom' (the so-called 'Wisdom that Has Gone Beyond'). Here we find a number of difficult texts of varying length. One very brief one, for instance, maintains that the whole teaching can be summed up in the letter A (Sanskrit, Ah). Another takes 100,000 verses to present it. The *Heart Sutra* and the *Diamond Sutra* are the best known and among the most concise texts.

All the texts are declaimed from the lokottara or transcendental point of view. That is, from a position of absolute non-duality, beyond all discriminative thought and verbal constructions. Viewed from this sublime vantage point, which is really no different from that of Enlightenment itself, there is no Buddha and no Enlightenment, no defilements and no purification, no production (of dharmas) and no extinction, no karma and no consequences of karma. There are no beings to be saved, therefore no bodhisattvas to save them. Form merges with emptiness, Samsara with Nirvana.

How can such things be? Well, the Buddha could not think 'I am the Buddha', for instance, for that would mean he had in his mind the idea of a person who possessed buddhahood. Being a buddha, he is at one with buddhahood: there is no duality. Therefore, for the Buddha there is no Buddha. Likewise 'Enlightenment' is an idea that occurs only to those who are not Enlightened. Indeed, they are a long way from it. It is 'those who do not consider whether they are far from Enlightenment, or near it' who are truly on course. And again, 'Nirvana' and 'Samsara' are only concepts in the minds of those who discriminate. For those who do not discriminate (that is, buddhas and bodhisattvas) 'Samsara and Nirvana become exactly the same.'

So all terms, including spiritually prestigious ones such as 'buddha', 'Enlightenment', 'bodhisattva', 'karma' and 'dharma', are just conventional constructions. Buddhas and bodhisattvas use them as skilful means to help suffering beings – though of course in an ultimate sense there are no beings and no suffering. Thus buddhas and bodhisattvas regard those whom they help as no more real than any army of phantoms conjured up by a skilful magician.

What then is the Prajñaparamita mode like? It can be compared, the texts say, to the vacuity and purity of space. The buddhas and bodhisattvas who 'course in it' take their stand nowhere and in nothing, neither in the conditioned nor the unconditioned. They seek no psychological supports, yet their position is diamond-solid. It will not crumble like Samsara and all its creations. For Samsara, it is continually emphasized, 'has no inner core':

As stars, a fault of vision, as a lamp,
A mock show, dew drops, or a bubble,
A dream, a lightning flash, or cloud,
So should one view what is conditioned.[3]

The Prajñaparamita exults in its own transcendental perspective and brings it poetically alive, while at the same time conspiring to strip us of all affirmations, all mental/verbal constructions, and drive us into the arms of that marvellous Beyond.

ABOVE *Prajñaparamita, goddess of wisdom.*

OPPOSITE *A page from the* Diamond Sutra, *one of the best known and most concise texts of the Mahayana teaching of Prajñaparamita.*

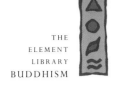

MADHYAMAKA
('Middle Way')

Tradition has it that the amorphous teachings of the Prajñaparamita were systematized by a sage named Nagarjuna (second century CE), the seminal master of the Madhyamaka or 'Middle Way' school. Highly celebrated, he is sometimes characterized as a second Buddha.

Though some have disputed his historicity, hagiography has it that Nagarjuna came from south Indian brahman stock. He brought to Mahayana Buddhism, not some creative new philosophical position, but a critical method that, if properly applied, would expunge all views and opinions by showing their ultimate absurdity, thereby at once restoring the mind to its native Prajñaparamita mode, free of all dualistic thought formations. As he himself says at the conclusion of the *Mulamadhyamaka-karika* ('Middle Way Verses'): 'I reverently bow to the Buddha who, out of compassion, has taught the true doctrine *in order to relinquish all views*.' So this is a philosophy that arrives at no conclusions. It in fact puts an end to all speculation and rumination – or, put another way, it probes the ultimate limits of what can be meaningfully thought and said. In this respect it resonates with the modern linguistic philosophy of Ludwig Wittgenstein.

Nagarjuna's method is described as dialectical: that is, it exploits the quirky, dualistic nature of language to turn all propositions on their heads. He uses various devices to this end, notably his famous tetralemma, by which a simple proposition may be reduced to four logical forms: 1 A; 2 not-A; 3 both A and not-A; and 4 neither A nor not-A. To take a concrete example: 1 Everything is real; 2 Everything is unreal; 3 Everything is both real and unreal; and 4 Everything is not real and not unreal.

The influence of Nagarjuna and his school was enormous. Stringent Madhyamaka became the dominant philosophy in Tibet and remained so until the Communist takeover in 1959. It was also successfully transmitted to both China and Japan, and is at present being enthusiastically studied in the West.

YOGACARA:
'Primacy of Consciousness'

Although Nagarjuna wanted to show the futility of all views, both positive and negative, the ruthless nature of his method – one writer calls it a kind of philosophical sadism – has a tendency to nihilism. As a counter to this negative disposition there later arose a more positive line – that taken by the masters of the Yogacara or Vijñāñavada school, who asserted the primacy of consciousness. The objects of the external world are not 'real' or external at all, they argued, but transformations of consciousness or mind. In support of this thesis they pointed to the fact that things can appear in the mind when there is no 'external' object present – in a dream, for instance, or through the practice of imaginative visualization.

In other schools this is known as the teaching of Citta-matra or 'Mind Only'. In the West it is called Idealism, the notion that only minds and mental events exist, which opposes Materialism, the notion that only matter exists.

Yogacara was not just a speculative philosophical school. As its name suggests, it was based on yoga practice. The philosophical aspect is therefore just upaya, skilful means, to point the devotee towards a profound insight that can only be gained through actual practice. This is the so-called 'revolution at the basis' (ashraya-paravritti). When a person finally sees that external objects are just projections of his own consciousness, he realizes that there is no object to be seized and no person to seize it. This leads to the Path of Insight that gives access to an ultimate state where perfect quiescence in a deep samadhi of pure consciousness supervenes.

RIGHT *Monks at Borobodur, on the island of Java in Indonesia. The domed stupas in the background are Buddhist monuments that usually contain sacred relics.*

THE HUA-YEN SCHOOL

The plethora of sacred texts that Buddhism produced was more than enough to perplex the ordinary mind. Understandably, then, attempts were made in mediaeval China to organize and classify the texts, indicating which the Buddha had prepared for those of high understanding and which for those of lesser understanding. Schools arose accordingly. In each case, one particular text was claimed to be pre-eminent: the Summa of the Buddha's teaching.

The T'ien t'ai (Japanese, Tendai) or White Lotus School was built around just such a project, its devotees venerating the *Saddharma-pundarika*.

Another was the Hua-yen or Flower Adornment School, its devotees preferring the *Avatamsaka Sutra*, a vast compilation of texts, some undoubtedly originating in India, probably put together in Central Asia in the third or fourth centuries CE.

In the last book of the *Avatamsaka*, the *Gandavyuha*, we are presented with the stunning Hua-yen vision of the Universe in which everything, down to the humblest item, includes everything else, in totality – open a speck of dust and you will find an entire universe! – and yet, paradoxically, nothing in any way foregoes its own special distinctiveness. Thus, any one item is the 'cause' of the whole Universe, and if it changes in even the most minute particular, the whole Universe changes too. Yet, in another and non-exclusive sense, that item is causally dependent on the totality.

So this is a grand panoramic vision of universal interdependence and interpenetration, hence popular among those with a 'green' or holistic cast of mind. It also cuts counter to the traditional Buddhist view of the world as an endless cycle of woes, for it positively affirms the world and all its constituents. Even the much-castigated human being, the creator and slave of egoism, the cockpit of passion, can hold his head up again! As one writer has aptly put it: 'In the Hua-yen Universe, everything counts!'

ZEN

Such rarefied philosophies as we have been briefly discussing of course stand in stark contrast to the noble silence that the Buddha is said to have maintained when plied with questions of a metaphysical or speculative nature. However useful, they only amount to head knowledge; and it is in fact very easy to be immensely learned about Buddhism (or anything else for that matter) in a scholastic way and be utterly unable to make the quantum leap to actualizing the teachings – making them live in our own daily lives.

The Zen school arose in China in the sixth century CE precisely to grapple with this problem. There were in the monasteries and temples Buddhist monks and nuns who had accumulated a great deal of head-knowledge. They had also steeped themselves in Buddhist morality and the monastic code of discipline. But they were stuck and could not make the necessary quantum leap. What the early Zen masters provided were powerful new methods – many of them iconoclastic by conventional Buddhist standards – for pushing practitioners beyond thought and discipline, up to a new octave-level where they could directly see into the great mystery of things for themselves.

Generally, the Zen school looks positively at the great mystery at the heart of things. '*What is it?*' is one of the classic questions that practitioners are urged to address with unremitting energy. Yet the early masters would brook no answer that smacked, however slightly, of conceptual thought. They demanded one that was existentially authentic: that came directly from the heart, from the human centre that enshrines the great mystery of man and the Universe.

All Buddhist teaching, then, insofar as it bears upon that great mystery, is a kind of circumambulation around it. Different doctrinal approaches are formulated to suit the unique circumstances of specific times and situations. Yet in the end we must let go of all thought and verbiage, let go of everything in fact, so that the great mystery may live through us.

OPPOSITE *An eighth-century banner from the Dunuang caves in China showing the Buddha preaching to his disciples.*

6

MORALITY

*I*n contemporary Western culture morals have become decidedly unfashionable.
This is largely because our own religious traditions have atrophied and their
ethical bases degenerated into rigid codes inimical to change, development and healthy
self-expression. On the other hand, living religious traditions, vitalized at source,
produce dynamic and relevant morals, and in the past these have provided the
springboards for great cultural advances.

So as a first practical step on the Buddhist path, we put our lives in good order. Just doing this in itself makes us feel better, less ill at ease with ourselves and less at odds with the world at large. We become more peaceful, more trusting, and that in turn causes good things to happen back to us – and to those around us. A two-way process.

Ideally, ethics should spring naturally from the heart, but in the first instance, at the beginner's stage, most of us need some kind of code to guide us, though it is always more important to keep to the spirit rather than the letter. The basic code that Buddhism offers is Pancha Sila or Five Precepts. Monks and nuns observe many additional rules: the Vinaya Pitaka of the Pali Canon, which is today still observed by Theravadins, lists some 227 rules for monks. For the laity, however, initially at least, just five are deemed sufficient:

1: Killing

Firstly, there is the principle to refrain from killing any living being. This of course includes the almost universal injunction against the murder of other human beings; but it also extends to include all kinds of other beings as well – animals, birds, fish and insects – for they too are spiritual beings like us, possessing the potential for spiritual growth, which includes of course the possibility of attaining human rebirth. Animals may also be regressed humans, for according to the Law of Karma it is possible for humans who have behaved badly to be reborn in that state – or as denizens of the other lower realms.

To be true to this principle and not collude in murder after the event, many Buddhists become vegetarians, though this is not obligatory. Early Buddhist monks, for instance, being mendicants, could accept meat that was put into their begging bowls. They were required to reject it only if they knew that its butchering had been done specifically for them. Some Mahayana schools were much more emphatic about vegetarianism, however.

Tantrists naturally have a different attitude. Meat actually figures as a sacrament in some of their rituals.

2: Theft and its Bedfellows

The second principle is to refrain from taking that which is not given. That is, stealing and its variants – including stealing from shops, 'borrowing' books and failing to return them, tax-dodging, and all kinds of other sharp practices, many of which have become socially acceptable in our go-getting society. In general, obtaining anything for oneself in ways that cause others to suffer is not morally sound, even if technically no law has been breached.

TOP *To Buddhists even insects, like the grasshopper, are spiritual beings.*

ABOVE *Women in Burma sweeping the ground so that monks can avoid stepping on and killing any insects.*

OPPOSITE *These Tibetan monks observe the Five Precepts as well as many other rules.*

3: Sex

The third principle is to refrain from irresponsible sexual activity: that is, activity that hurts others in any way.

As the strongest passion to which we are prone, sex is always highly charged karmically. It can cause all sorts of things to happen, not least that a new life enters this world. It must therefore be regulated, but at the same time it cannot be safely repressed. As the thirteenth-century Japanese Zen monk-poet Yoshida Kenko wrote:

The passion of love is deep-rooted; its true source is a great mystery. There are desires connected with all the senses; all but this may be conquered. No-one is exempt; young and old, wise and foolish alike are its slaves. It is a terrible madness, one to be dreaded – yet one for which we should never reproach another.[1]

All sexual activity is of course proscribed for Buddhist monks and nuns, but it is understood that lay people will have sex lives – though, of course, this is not obligatory! Celibacy is quite a healthy state, providing it does not involve repressing, that is, a denial or thwarting of the libido whereby it is thrust below consciousness. On the matter of sex, however, one must say that generally Buddhism is not very positive. In the spectrum of religions it is way over on the ascetic, body-denying, monastic wing – the opposite, in fact of Judaism and Islam, which seeks to integrate sexuality into worldly and spiritual life. The Buddhist sutras and other works speak very disparagingly of this very natural instinct, basically because it was seen as the primary means whereby people become entrammelled in family life, which affords restricted opportunities for spiritual practice.

BELOW *A Tantric statue of Vajrasattva, who personifies purity and ultimate reality, embracing a consort. Tantra, unlike other forms of Buddhism, advocates the positive use of sexual energy as a means of gaining Enlightenment.*

In general, the Buddhist message would seem to be: if you are serious about living the spiritual life, it is best to have transcended sex. The exception again of course is Tantra, which characteristically takes its stance at the opposite pole and seeks to integrate sexuality – indeed to use sexual energy as a means for gaining Enlightenment. Some modern Western Buddhists, such as Alan Watts, have also sought a similar integration, and understandably so, for as the psychologist C G Jung has pointed out, spirituality and sexuality have for too long been at odds, not just in Buddhism but generally, and a reconciliation is called for. Given that Buddhism is a non-dogmatic and dynamic religion that adapts to meet changing conditions, it may well be that this kind of reconciliation is something that will be attempted and achieved before too long – and probably in the West.

4: Speech

The penultimate principle is to refrain from harmful misuse of the faculty of speech. These include lying, slander, malicious or idle gossip, misrepresentation, blackmail and so forth. Obviously these can cause pain to others and create disharmony. There is also another reason: if we are really serious about living the spiritual life (or even a sane worldly life) we must keep a firm grip on truth, on what is the case, otherwise we may all too easily lose our bearings and fall victim to the many pitfalls with which the path is beset. We must most of all be clear about our own motivation – a kind of inner 'right speech'.

Sadly, in our culture truth is being debased all the time. We have politicians who lie and high officials who admit that they have been 'economical with the truth'. We have phenomena such as 'creative accountancy' and, in public relations, we have elevated the manipulation of facts and figures and people's minds into a high (and highly rewarded) art.

5: Drink and drugs

The final principle is to refrain from ingesting substances that befuddle consciousness. This includes alcoholic drink and the whole gamut of dope. Not only do these lead to heedless activity but they also impede awareness and, as we shall see in the next chapter on meditation, the development of awareness or clear-seeing is essential. Drink and drugs are also often avenues of escape from the dark and difficult things of life, including our own personal problems.

Of course, the monastic codes make drink and drugs absolutely off-limits for monks and nuns, but Tantra yet again has its own antinomian attitude to these things, and in lay circles in the West today things also differ from the patterns established in the East. In our cold, northerly lands, ale has traditionally been a staple beverage, spirits a comforter and wine a sacrament. Many Western Buddhists, therefore, are not averse to a moderate amount of social drinking – moderate being the operative term here – though many others still prefer to abstain completely.

Something must also be said about drugs. Since the 1960s, many genuine spiritual searchers have experimented with consciousness-raising drugs such as LSD, cannabis, peyote and mescalin, and claim to have received profound experiences under their influence. Whether such experiences are really spiritual has been questioned; and in any case they do not produce lasting changes – only sustained practice can do that. There are also identifiable dangers connected with specific drugs, and the fact that they are illegal surrounds them with a paranoid ambience. However, no conclusive evidence for their spiritual relevance or irrelevance exists as little dispassionate research has been done.

These Five Precepts should not be regarded as grave and rigid laws. The Buddha did not want to make us guilt-ridden or turn us into rigid fundamentalists who grasp the letter of the law but miss the spirit. A lot of disharmony and suffering can be generated by stickling demands for strict adherence to principle, whereas a little good-hearted flexibility can make for more harmony and less complication.

The precepts, then, are in the nature of ideals or guidelines, to be used with flexibility and good sense. If we fail to live up to any of them, we should not torment ourselves with visions of hellish punishments. Rather we should learn from our failure and resolve to do better in future. Nor should morality be used as a stick with which to beat others. The moderately wise person attends to his or her own faults, attempting to rectify them, and does not preoccupy him or herself overly with the faults of others.

The Environment

We can see that implicit in all five precepts is the age-old Indian principle of ahimsa: *not harming* – either others or oneself. We can safely extend this to the environment, the world as a whole and even to outer space. Nothing in fact falls outside the sphere of our moral responsibility. For instance, according to the Hua-yen school of Buddhist philosophy, which developed in mediaeval China, our every action affects the *whole* of the Universe.

The grave environmental problems we now face on Planet Earth stem directly from our ignorance of this fact. Yet even as we begin to see what we are doing and what suffering it will bring down on both ourselves and our descendants, we find it very difficult to change our ways.

Right Livelihood

Additional to the five moral precepts outlined in this chapter, in the Noble Eightfold Path, an early graduated scheme of the way to Enlightenment, we find mention of Right Livelihood. This means earning our living in ways that do not harm, deprive or exploit other people, animals and the environment. The modern obsession with economic growth has, however, produced a culture where anything goes as long as it makes money.

7

MEDITATION

We live our lives in a kind of waking dream. We are only hazily aware of what is really going on both outside and, even more so, inside ourselves. It needs a vital shock, like a stark confrontation with death, to jerk us awake. Then for a moment the scales of semi-sleep, subjectivity, projection and fantasy fall from our eyes and we see the world as it really is.

Meditation is about developing that kind of acute awareness all the time. And it means doing so without becoming attached to the objects of observation out of desire, or rejecting them from aversion. It means becoming the dispassionate watcher, the one who knows: becoming buddha, in fact. Buddhism traditionally calls it Smrti (Pali, Sati): Mindfulness.

MINDFULNESS

The basic form of meditation that the early texts describe the Buddha as teaching is not sitting meditation, as one might have expected from modern formal practice, but something to be done by a monk as he goes about his normal business. It consists of the specific applications of Mindfulness, described by the Buddha in the *Satipatthana Sutta*:

There is this one way, monks, for the purification of beings, for the overcoming of sorrow and griefs, for the going down of suffering and miseries, for realizing Nirvana; that is to say, the four applications of mindfulness. What are the four? A monk fares along contemplating the body in the body, ardent, clearly conscious of it, mindful of it so as to control covetousness and dejection in the world; he fares along contemplating the feelings in the feelings, the mind in the mind, and the mental objects in the mental objects, ardent, clearly conscious of them, mindful of them so as to control covetousness and dejection in the world.[1]

Although it is emphasized in this text that Mindfulness should be established 'precisely to the extent necessary just for knowledge, just for remembrance' and 'independently of and not grasping anything in the world', its application should be wide and deep and along prescribed lines. For instance, when in contemplation of the body, the practitioner should not be merely aware of his present posture or any action he may be performing; he should also at appropriate times reflect upon the nature of the body – the fact that it is like a skin bag containing various impurities, organs, bones and so on. Special emphasis is laid on the gruesome aspects of the physical body, and if he passes a cemetery the practitioner is urged to reflect that his body too is of the same nature as those that now lie there 'swollen, discoloured, decomposing'. In this way, attachment to the body is undermined.

The benefits to be obtained from this practice are very high: 'either profound knowledge here-now, or, if there is any residuum remaining, the state of non-returning' (that is, the state of a being who rises to a higher world and reaches Nirvana without being reborn in this world again).

SHAMATHA(*'Calm Abiding'*)and VIPASHYANA (*'Insight'*)

Later systematizers and the compilers of Buddhist meditation manuals subdivided meditation practice into two parts: Shamatha (Calm Abiding) and Vipashyana (Insight or Higher Vision). In the Pali language they are known as Shamatha and Vipassana.

Shamatha is concerned with developing concentration – that is, the ability to maintain the focus of attention one-pointedly but without undue exertion on a chosen object – and with calming and stabilizing the mind so that it is no longer disturbed by deluding excitations.

The establishment of these qualities of calmness and concentration are vital preliminaries for Vipashyana practice, which is the more active analysis and investigation of all phenomena that fall within the ambit of consciousness (these too are enumerated in some detail in the texts) with a view to a penetrative realization of their true nature.

Shamatha may release paranormal powers, known as *siddhis*. These classically include the ability to heal, to read people's characters (or minds) and foretell the future, to levitate and raise bodily temperature by many degrees at will, walk on water, multiply the body infinitely – and so forth. It is always emphasized, however, that these are by-products of spiritual practice, not objectives, and if they arise great care should be taken not to be seduced by them.

It is also possible to enter the dhyanas and samapattis, the so-called trance states and formless absorptions. These are eight increasingly rarefied states of mind in which sense perceptions and thoughts are progressively eliminated and consciousness becomes more and more subtle until merely the slightest residue remains. At the very apex of the system the practitioner may indeed enter a ninth absorption, Nirodha-samapatti (complete cessation of thought and consciousness), which is an experience of Nirvana-like bliss lasting for up to seven days.

Some practitioners practise Shamatha assiduously in order to enter the dhyanas and the samapattis, and the text-books recommend the use of special objects of concentration (kasina), such as coloured discs, for this purpose. But while all this may be interesting, it can also be another trap. Seduced by the bliss to be enjoyed in those subtle states, the practitioner can all too easily be stripped of all motivation to push on to the true end of the spiritual project, Enlightenment itself, which can only be attained through Vipashyana.

In Vipashyana or Insight Meditation, the calmness and concentrative ability forged in Shamatha are used to inquire penetratively into the true nature of things. Intense observation and analysis of phenomena encountered will, according to the classic texts, reveal that all are subject to duhkha, anitya and anatman, and are inherently painful or unsatisfactory, impermanent and devoid of atman or self – or put simply: 'everything that arises passes away and is not self.' This is not mere head-knowledge but a deep existential understanding that is at once purifying and liberating. More positively, it is said to also give access to the Unconditioned: to Nirvana.

RIGHT Contemplating a gravel garden. Meditation helps to calm the mind and leads to deeper understanding of the true nature of things.

OPPOSITE Meditation by Moonlight by Yoshitoshi (1839–92).

Basic Meditation: How to Practise

Most practitioners sit on the floor on a small, plump cushion. They assume the classic cross-legged lotus or half-lotus position. If this is not possible, a straight-backed chair will do. The important thing is to keep the back straight (though not stiff or rigid) and the head balanced on the upright neck. The hands should be laid loosely in the lap, one lying inside the other or holding the other firmly. The eyes are then half closed and the arrow of attention turned inwards.

Now, letting go of all active preoccupations (planning, problem-solving, scheming, fantasizing and so on), we come fully into the here-now. Just allow yourself to relax alertly into the aware state. This state is not something we have to create. It is the ground of our being; all we have to do then is allow it gently to come into its own. So there should be no goal-oriented striving or forcing, only the exertion of sufficient energy to prevent us from lapsing into an empty sleep-like or day-dreaming state.

Next, steer awareness towards a particular object. Usually the rise and fall of the breath is recommended. Watch how it passes in and out of the nostrils, or watch the rise and fall of the diaphragm.

Or you can concentrate on the 'fire-field' of the tanden, the area some five centimetres below the navel – whatever is most comfortable.

Of course in the beginning – and indeed for a long time afterwards, for that matter – it is very difficult to keep awareness on target. The mind, accustomed for so long to its own wayward habits, will tend to wander away and be caught and excited by any thought that happens to stray into its ambit – and so off into the endless labyrinths of rumination. But now you can make a start at breaking this vicious cycle. Gradually you will experience moments when the mind is marvellously calm and clear, the heart at peace – but only temporarily ... the old turmoil will relentlessly return, time and time again. You must not be discouraged, however, or think you are a bad meditator. Meditation is one area where judgement or competition is right out of place. Instead just go back to the basic breath-watching practice and patiently persist with it. Also do not allow yourself to become attached to those wonderful moments of calmness and clarity, or contrive to reconstruct them. Attachment and striving will only inhibit their return. All you can do is go on, doing the best you can. There are in fact traditionally said to be five 'hindrances' that impede progress in meditation. They are sensual desires, ill-will (or aversion), laziness, restlessness and worry, and doubt.

Because most of us do not normally like to confront ourselves honestly, when we begin to open up the mind in meditation a great deal of repressed or forgotten material – what Jung would call aspects of our Shadow or Dark Side – will often rise into consciousness, sometimes disturbingly. If this happens, you should again observe that material, not getting caught up with it but certainly not trying to suppress it. For here you have a rare chance to undergo very effective psychotherapy. If you hospitably allow it, however dark or disturbing it may be, to enter consciousness and rest there, in full awareness, it will in time fade away quite naturally. Then you will learn the great truth that your biggest bogies – your deepest fears, guilts and pains; your most distressing problems – are no more substantial than the morning dew. Awareness, like the sun, will evaporate them.

LEFT *A Burmese sculpture of the Buddha.*

❧

OPPOSITE *An ivory statue on a turquoise matrix from the Ming Dynasty (1368–1644). The Buddha is typically depicted sitting in meditation in the lotus position.*

Meditation on Loving-Kindness

Although the meditation techniques employed in Basic Buddhism, compared with those developed later, tend to be relatively simple and passive, there are some quite active forms. For instance, it is possible to use the so-called Brahma Viharas or 'Heavenly Abodes' as objects of concentration in Shamatha practice. The Viharas include loving-kindness (maitri), compassion (karuna), sympathetic joy (mudita) and equanimity (upeksha). The sending out of maitri to individuals in need – and in ever increasing circles, to the whole duhkha-torn world – is particularly favoured by modern Western practitioners.

This is a typical quotation from the sutras:

There, O monks, the monk with a mind full of loving-kindness pervading first one direction, then a second one, then a third one, then a fourth one, just so above, below and all around; and everywhere identifying himself with all, he is pervading the whole world with mind full of loving-kindness, with mind wide, developed, unbounded, free from hate and ill-will.[2]

It is also important that we direct loving-kindness to ourselves, for if we do not like ourselves, how can we like – let alone love – others?

Although this practice clearly embodies a concentrative element, it is also very much about generating particular kinds of thoughts and feelings, and so may fall a little outside what purists might regard as meditation. In other words, it has form, whereas 'true' meditation, it might be argued, is formless – or as nearly formless as possible. Yet within the early Buddhism schools – and indeed the later ones – texts on meditation enumerate long lists of worthy subjects upon which the calm and concentrated mind is encouraged to ponder deeply.

ABOVE *A Buddhist monk in the temple grounds in Thailand. The peaceful surroundings and beauty of the temple are conducive to meditation practices.*

MAHAYANA BUDDHIST MEDITATION

Mahayana Buddhism, of course, has rather different objectives from those of the early schools. The devotees of the Mahayana aspire to a similar profound penetration of the truth of Shunyata, Emptiness, and make this a primary object of meditation. They also seek to generate bodhisattvic qualities so that they can work effectively in Samsara to alleviate the suffering of sentient beings. Yet for all that, the meditation methods of most Mahayana schools rest firmly on a basis of Mindfulness and Shamatha-Vipashyana.

For instance, the early masters of the Yogacara school employed the Buddha's classic application of mindfulness method – again in a manner not restricted to the meditation cushion – though they made subtle adaptations to suit their own outlook and purposes. According to the great Vasubandhu, whereas the early Buddhists are mindful of merely their own bodies, etc., the bodhisattvas are mindful in two directions: both of their own and others' bodies, etc.; and the bodhisattvas practise in this way, not merely to cultivate non-attachment but 'neither for lack of attachment, nor for non-lack of attachment, but for a Nirvana which has no abode'.[3]

The seminal masters of the T'ien-t'ai school, which originated in China and whose devotees regard the *Lotus Sutra* as the Summa of the Buddha's teachings, also had their own distinctive views about Shamatha-Vipashyana. Chih-i (sixth century) maintained that Shamatha practice (Chinese, chih) could produce insight into Shunyata but of an imperfect, reclusive and passive sort. This could be corrected by Vipashyana practice (Chinese, kuan), which would, among other things, afford deeper insight into the true nature of things and generate practical bodhisattvic compassion. Taken together chih and kuan could bring about compassionate wisdom in which all phenomena could be seen as neither real nor unreal.

The T'ien-t'ai school was renowned for its meditation practices, which it classified according to a gradual, sudden and perfect paradigm. Four ways of attaining samadhi or one-pointed concentration was also delineated. These included meditation for 90 days on a proper subject (such as the Buddha); circumambulation of a statue of the compassionate Buddha, Amitabha, for 90 days, and/or invocation of his Holy Name; 90 days of sitting and walking practice aimed at rooting out defilements; and concentration upon Emptiness and the other characteristics of Ultimate Reality.

BELOW *Buddha carved in the cliff face in China.*

ZEN MEDITATION

The Zen school, known in China as Ch'an, might be called the meditation school par excellence. Ostensibly disparaging scriptural learning (though in fact squarely rooted in Yogacara and Prajñaparamita philosophy) and other practices (such as performing rituals, reciting the scriptures, and so on), Zen meditation emphasizes direct seeing into one's own nature.

Soto Zen meditation is usually practised facing a blank wall. The internal method – sticklers would no doubt call it a non-method – is essentially formless. Dogen, who transmitted the teachings of the school from China to Japan, declares that zazen (sitting meditation) is not about learning to do concentration. It is not introspection. It is not thinking of good or bad. It is not a conscious endeavour of any kind. There should not be expectations. One should not even desire to become a buddha. Just –

Sit solidly in meditation and think not-thinking. How do you think not-thinking? Nonthinking. This is the art of zazen.[4]

In this, practice and realization are not separate. Just to sit is to be a buddha.

Meditation in the Rinzai tradition, on the other hand, is rather more militant. Practitioners sit in straight lines, facing each other. They begin perhaps with a Shamatha-type breath-watching or counting practice to bring about calmness and concentration. Then they traditionally apply themselves with concentrated effort to koan practice.

Koan riddles (Chinese, kung-an) are generally based on the records of real life situations in which early masters enlightened their students. In Sung dynasty China, as Zen began to lose its original flair and vitality, these were collected in great anthologies such as the *Blue Cliff Record* and the *Gateless Gate*. These formalized riddles, now having something of the significance of precedents in case law, are still handed out to Rinzai Zen

practitioners today. Pondering them long and deeply, the students will attempt to give an 'answer' to the teacher, usually in Japan called a roshi or 'old master', in the course of regular interviews (sanzen). The roshi will then judge its authenticity. Any 'answer' that smacks, however slightly, of conceptualization or phoney contrivance will be ruthlessly rejected. If, however, the devotee comes up with an acceptable answer, he or she may well be adjudged to have had a genuine breakthrough or satori. But that is just the beginning. More work must be done to deepen understanding. In other words, once a degree of calmness, clarity and concentration has been produced, the koan is an extremely active device for continually throwing the student against the ultimate question of his own nature.

OPPOSITE *Tanka of the Shakyamuni Buddha surrounded by various gods.*

BELOW LEFT *A rare painting of the thirteenth-century Japanese Zen Master Dogen.*

TANTRIC MEDITATION

Buddhist Tantra aims at bringing about Enlightenment very speedily by special yogic means. It is not, however, according to its own teachings, suited to everyone. Only special candidates who have already practised long and successfully, gained deep insight into Shunyata (Emptiness) as well as having developed a high degree of bodhicitta qualify to practise it. Then they must forge a connection with a learned guru, who will initiate them into the mandala or sacred precinct of their chosen deity (yidam). The rite of initiation (abhisheka) that the guru bestows allows the devotee to perform a range of specialized rituals and practices (sadhana), many of which involve working with dark aspects of the psyche. Herein lie special dangers, so to protect both the unwary from burning themselves and the teachings from being debased, Tantra is hedged around with a veil of secrecy, grave vows and other protections.

Buddhist Tantra possesses an extensive pantheon of yidam or deities. Some, such as Avalokiteshvara, the Bodhisattva of Compassion, his female Tibetan form of Tara, and Mañjushri, the Bodhisattva of Wisdom, wielder of the adamantine sword that slices away all delusion, are benign. Others, such as Yamantaka, Mahakala and Chakrasamvara, are wrathful. All probably developed from ancient non-Buddhist Indian deities. Chakrasamvara, for instance, is a Buddhist transformation of Shiva, the ascetic-erotic Hindu deity of death and regeneration.

Insofar as Tantra involves meditation it presupposes a solid basis in Mindfulness and Shamatha-Vipashyana (known in Tibetan as Shine-Lhatong). Given these, its own distinctive practices involve creative visualization, which is carried out to a virtuoso degree of proficiency. The devotee will learn, for instance, to create the form of his chosen deity out of the bija or seed mantra that embodies the essence of the deity, the bija being firstly created out of the Emptiness of his own mind. The mental image of the deity

ABOVE LEFT *The four-armed Avalokiteshvara, the Bodhisattva of Compassion, one of the Tantric deities.*

LEFT *Buddha holding a vajra, symbolising the energy of the mantra, in which personal power is stored.*

MEDITATION

must be built up in very precise detail and full colour according to archetypal patterns.

The Tantric yogi aims eventually to acquire the enlightened qualities of his yidam – which are really his own innate enlightened qualities. While this might be quite understandable in the case of benign deities, it is perhaps far less easy to understand in the case of wrathful ones, which in traditional iconography were depicted as extremely macabre beings with bloodshot eyes and flaring fangs, sporting necklaces of skulls, carrying skull-caps and daggers, and surrounded by wreaths of fire. Some passionately couple with their shakti consorts – a symbol both of the union of wisdom and skilful means, and of the bliss of the Enlightenment which that union produces. For according to the Buddhist view such dark and passionate energies, when purified, also possess enlightened qualities.

At the apogee of Tibetan Buddhist Tantra lies Highest Yoga Tantra (Anuttara Yoga Tantra), which has two stages. The purpose of the first stage, the Generation Stage, is to practise transformation of the death, intermediate (or bardo) and birth stages into the path. This prepares the Tantric yogi for the Completion Stage, where he will work with the subtle body. This consists of a number of centres (chakra) and channels (nadi), through which a 'wind-energy' (lung) circulates. In unreconstructed beings, because the channels are knotted up the circulation of the wind-energy is disrupted, resulting in our gross and deluded behaviour. The yogi, however, will consciously direct the wind-energy directly up through the chakras to the infinitesimal 'droplet' (bindu) in the heart chakra. This will purify and separate the subtle body from the gross body. Discursive thought is instantly expunged and the primordial enlightened state supervenes.

ABOVE RIGHT *An illustration from Rajasthan, c1700, also depicting the secret celestial upper chakras and channels of the subtle body.*

RIGHT *Tara, the female Tibetan form of Avalokiteshvara.*

THE PRINCIPAL
SCHOOLS AND TRADITIONS

ABOVE *Thai monks. Buddhists in Sri Lanka, Burma and
Thailand tend to follow the Theravada tradition.*

1: THERAVADA BUDDHISM

Tracing its roots back to the seminal Sthaviravada school that arose in India after the Buddha's death, the devotees of the Theravada or 'Way of the Elders' would argue that their tradition is the true repository of the teachings and practices propagated by Shakyamuni himself. In their eyes it therefore stands as a fixed pole of orthodoxy and tradition amidst the mêlée of 2,500 years of change and development. Others would, however, dispute this, arguing that the Theravada is itself a very much later development and that consequently it can make no claims to special priority.

Whatever the truth of the matter, the Theravada survives today as a living tradition in Sri Lanka, Burma and Thailand, and it is from these countries that it has been transmitted to the West. The Pali Canon is still very much its scriptural foundation, and the Pali language rather than Sanskrit is used for chanting and other liturgical purposes. A lively tradition of Pali scholarship exists, also an active tradition of meditation. In the East, while the scholar-monks tend to gravitate to the larger temples and monasteries where facilities exist for their work, the dedicated meditators are more likely to seek out secluded places. These 'forest monks' may live in outlying monasteries or else alone in caves or huts like the early Sangha (Community). Some wander from place to place, accepting whatever in the way of food or shelter may be offered to them – or not offered. This is regarded as a form of dhutanga or hard practice, and is considered to be particularly beneficial for shaking off the defilements.

As a sign of their renunciation of worldly values, monks and nuns shave off their facial and cranial hair, and wear the traditional ochre or orange robe. Having committed themselves to a life of poverty and mendicancy, they have few possessions, but one essential is a bowl into which lay devotees may put food. They also vow themselves to chastity, and the most scrupulous will neither carry nor touch money. All strive hard not to be idle or to fritter energy away in self-indulgences, such as unnecessary sleep or gratuitous chatter. Bounded as they are at all times by their numerous precepts and rules, they have in any case to be constantly mindful of what they are doing and able to accept a very high degree of circumscription. Hierarchy is important too. When addressing those senior to them – that is, those who were ordained earlier than they were – monks should bow and generally show due respect.

BELOW *Monks in an alms procession in Sri Lanka.*

BOTTOM *Ritual shaving of novitiate Burmese monks as part of their initiation into religious life.*

Monastic Life

At the European Theravadin monastery that I visit, the monks get up very early – at 4am – and go to the shrine-room, where they chant for some time before the great gilded image of the Buddha, then sit in silent meditation. According to the rules, they are only allowed to eat between dawn and noon. They therefore have a simple breakfast of plain rice gruel and tea. Afterwards chores are done, and some monks will leave on the daily alms round (Pali, pindapad), taking their begging bowls with them. As food donated by the laity is prepared in the monastery kitchen by lay-brothers (anagarika) and laity, this Oriental tradition might be thought unnecessary. However, it is maintained out of respect for tradition and also so that the community can keep in touch with the local people. The substantial meal of the day is duly taken before 12 noon, then there is a period of rest before the afternoon work-session begins. Tea is taken in the late afternoon, plus certain allowable 'medicines' such as cheese or black chocolate. Then at 7.30pm it is back to the shrine-room for more chanting and silent meditation. At about 9pm monks and nuns are free to go to bed, but must be ready to rise again when the bell rings at 4am.

This austere daily routine goes on year in, year out, punctuated only by periods of retreat when the community draws together for more intensive practice. Some monks or nuns may also embark on solitary retreats, or go off on dhutanga – the 'hard practice' mentioned earlier, when they wander from place to place, usually in the West accompanied by a lay-brother or a layman. There may also be visits to schools, local Buddhist societies and other places to deliver discourses (Pali, desana) and/or lead meditation.

Within this particular community, any person wishing to take the robe has first to serve a probationary period of at least one year as an anagarika. He or she then shaves both head and face, dons a white robe and lives by eight precepts – that is, the Five Precepts of Buddhism plus three additional ones: not to eat at wrong times; to refrain from dancing, singing and music, attending shows, wearing garlands and using perfumes and cosmetics; and not to lie on a high or luxurious bed. In addition he or she will be encouraged to take on board some 75 rules of etiquette.

His term as an anagarika completed, a man may request to be given the monk's precepts – 227 of them in all, though only about 20 are of practical significance today – at a ceremony held before the annual Vassa or Rains Retreat in a sima or consecrated space. He will then be able to wear the ochre (or orange) robe. A woman, on the other hand, cannot become a fully-fledged nun (Pali, bhikkhuni) as the order of nuns has technically died out, but she may take the vows of a Dasa Sila Mata or Ten Precept Sister, which is what we mean by 'nun' in the present context. This is done at a ceremony in the shrine-room when she will exchange the white robe for a brown one. She is then bound by the eight precepts listed above, of which the seventh, concerning dancing, singing, and so on, is divided in two, plus an additional precept prohibiting the handling of money, gold and silver. She will also take on numerous training rules. Four rules, known in Pali as Parajika Offences, are considered especially grave and anyone transgressing them would be expelled from the order and not allowed to rejoin. These concern sexual intercourse, deliberate killing, deliberate stealing and claiming to possess paranormal powers. All the rules are rehearsed by the whole community twice monthly on Uposatha days.

A life circumscribed by so many rules, which drastically curtail personal liberty and self-expression, might seem a very bleak prospect. Many who have actually lived it, however, report that after initial struggles they actually begin to feel more free – free in particular from the burden of self and its endless conflicts and demands. This leads at times to the welling up of great joy and a sense of serenity. Of course, if the life does not prove suitable, a monk or nun may leave at any time by handing their robes back to their preceptor, though as this is regarded as a serious step they will be counselled first and asked to pause before making a final decision. Leaving does not, however, debar anyone from seeking reordination later.

TOP RIGHT *Buddhist monks in Thailand
on their morning rounds for food.*

MIDDLE RIGHT *Buddhist nuns in Burma.*

BELOW RIGHT *Buddhist monks in
a British monastery receiving food from
lay people.*

The traditional relationship between Theravadin monastics and laity is one of useful symbiosis. The monastery is the spiritual focus of the locality in which it is situated. Monks live and practise there, and the laity may come to stay for a period of retreat or just for a brief visit. Uposatha days – full and half moon days – and festivals draw large crowds of lay devotees, who come with dana (gifts), including food to offer to the monks and nuns. Afterwards there may be a communal meal and there is usually much conviviality. There will be a certain amount of ritual too: chanting from the Pali scriptures is usual, the delivery of a blessing, a discourse from the abbot, perhaps a period of silent reflection, and the recitation of the Five Precepts. The Three Refuges may also be taken when, led by the monastics, the laity will chant a Pali formula. Taking refuge in this way is an important rite, affirming or reaffirming one's faith in Buddha, Dharma and Sangha.

Special ceremonies are also carried out at monasteries to celebrate rites of passage – birth, marriage and death.

The principal Theravada festivals include the celebration of the Buddha's Birth, Enlightenment and Parinirvana – called Wesak in the Sri Lankan tradition, Vaisakha Puja in the Thai – on the full moon day of May; and Kathina in October or November, which celebrates the ending of the three-month Rains Retreat when monks withdraw into their monastery for intensive practice. At Kathina the laity bring special gifts for the Sangha, notably cloth for robes.

2: TIBETAN BUDDHISM

The Tantric Buddhism of Tibet could not stand in stronger contrast to the Theravada. When travellers familiar only with the Southern School first encountered it they thought that if indeed it was Buddhism then it could only represent a fall from the high spiritual standards set by the Buddha.

To walk into a Tibetan temple is to be confronted by raw primary colours – red, blue, green, mustard – the mingled aromas of strong incense and butter lamps, the benign and wrathful deities depicted on scroll paintings hanging on the walls or painted on the walls themselves, and a rich array of gilded figures and votive objects. If there are lamas present, one may hear the monotonous, guttural drone of their chanting, periodically augmented perhaps by the cacophonous clash of cymbals and the wailing of thigh-bone trumpets and other instruments. Here are suggestions of magic and mystery that resonate with something suppressed and half-forgotten in the depths of our being.

Their seclusion on the Roof of the World enabled the Tibetans to preserve the Mahayana and Tantric Buddhism of India for over a millennium and to create a uniquely rich spiritual culture. Unfortunately in 1950 the Chinese Communists felt the need to 'liberate' these people from the thrall of Western imperialism. Despite the fact that there were virtually no Westerners – and certainly no imperialists – in Tibet at the time, the Chinese went ahead … and became imperialists themselves, taking over the government of what had hitherto effectively been an autonomous nation, colonizing it, plundering its mineral and natural wealth, and making the Tibetans themselves virtual aliens in their own land. The Tibetans voted with their feet against this 'liberation', and when the Chinese finally – and bloodily – completed their takeover in 1959, tens of thousands fled to exile in India. The virtual destruction of Buddhism in Tibet was completed during the Cultural Revolution (1966–76).

Yet these violent and destructive events did have one positive outcome: they made the spiritual riches of Tibetan Buddhism accessible to Westerners for the first time. After 1959, lamas – including HH the Dalai Lama – began to visit the West, and Tibetan Buddhist centres were set up. Today we can claim that four major schools are well established on Western soil.

LEFT *A Tibetan tanka of the Avoloketesvara with Mañjushri and Vajrapani.*

The Nyingma School

The Nyingmapa[1] are less inclined to monasticism and decidedly more inclined to magic. They particularly venerate the Tantric adept Padmasambhava (Guru Rinpoche). Having overcome the occult forces inimical to it, he successfully transmitted Buddhism to Tibet in the seventh century CE.

The Sakya School

The school's most important doctrinal and meditational cycle is *The Path and its Fruit*, a systematization of both Sutra (that is, pre-Tantric) and Tantric teachings credited to the ninth-century Indian adept Virupa and based on the *Hevajra Tantra*. According to Ngakpa Jampa Thaye (David Stott):

> *The philosophical viewpoint which informs* The Path and its Fruit *is the notion of the inseparability of Samsara and Nirvana ... It is said: 'By abandoning Samsara one will realize Nirvana.' Mind itself, the union of Luminosity and Emptiness, is the root of Samsara and Nirvana. When obscured it takes the form of Samsara and when freed of obscurations it is Nirvana. The key to Buddhahood, the ultimate source of benefit for all beings, lies in this realization.*[2]

By following this path one can apparently attain Enlightenment in a single life.

LEFT Religious wall painting in the Dalai Lama's palace in Tibet. The Tantric Buddhism of Tibet has a rich tradition of elaborate religious art.

The Kagyu School

Practical mysticism rather than bookish scholarship characterizes the Kagyu school – 'Kagyu' literally meaning 'Transmitted Command'.

The most famous disciple and heir to the Kagyu lineage was Milarepa (1052–1135), who, because he had foolishly dabbled in black magic, had also to be put through an extremely rigorous course of training. Never ordaining as a monk and avoiding institutions, Milarepa became the much-loved prototype of the freewheeling yogi who pursues his own spontaneous spiritual path in lonely places. He gained many wonderful powers as a result of his austerities and was able on one occasion to defeat a priest of the Bön religion in a contest of magic for the possession of Mount Kailas, the great sacred mountain in Western Tibet. He was a poet too.

Milarepa's most influential disciple was the 'Doctor of Takpo', Gampopa (1079–1153), author of the classic text *The Jewel Ornament of Liberation*.

The Gelug School

As its name – Gelug means 'Virtuous' – suggests, this began as a reform movement initiated by Tsongkhapa (1357–1419; also known as Jé Rinpoche), a pious monk from north-eastern Tibet. He stressed the importance of a basis of ethics and, for monks, the monastic virtues (strict celibacy, abstention from intoxicants and so forth), and he encouraged study so that practitioners might obtain a clear intellectual understanding of the nature and aim of the Buddhist path. He felt particularly strongly that a firm grounding in the Sutra teachings should be obtained before any attempt was made to negotiate the heady world of Tantra.

Tsongkhapa's chief disciples founded the Gelug school, which enjoyed both spiritual and temporal pre-eminence in Tibet from the sixteenth century down to 1959. It was the Mongols, the original patrons of the school, who bestowed the title 'Dalai Lama' on its third head, 'Dalai' meaning 'Ocean (of Wisdom)', and also retroactively on his predecessors back to Gendundrup, putative nephew and disciple of Tsongkhapa. The present incumbent, the fourteenth, is the monk Tenzin Gyatso, born in 1935 in eastern Tibet but presently living in Dharamsala, his 'capital-in-exile' in the foothills of the Indian Himalaya. The Fourteenth Dalai Lama's great spiritual qualities, his warmth and cheerfulness, and the way in which he has led his people through one of the most difficult periods of their history, always advocating a non-violent response to Chinese violations in Tibet, won him the Nobel Peace Prize in 1989. He is, along with the Fifth and the Thirteenth, one of the great Dalai Lamas.

OPPOSITE *The Fourteenth Dalai Lama.*

BELOW *The Abbot of a Mongolian temple destroyed in the 1930s. The Mongols were the original patrons of the Gelug school.*

The Lama in Tibetan Buddhism

It is hard to overestimate the importance of the lama in the Tibetan tradition. The word means a guru or teacher, who may be either married or a celibate monk, though not all monks (gelong) teach. The commentary to Tsongkhapa's *Foundation of All Excellence* explains that 'the very root to Enlightenment is the practice of reliance on a spiritual teacher.' It goes on:

*Having realized that the spiritual teacher
is the root of all excellence, by continuous effort
of body, speech and mind, develop great faith that
recognizes his knowledge and does not observe in
him the slightest fault. Remember his vast
kindness with deep gratitude, and honour him;
make offerings to him, respect him in body
and speech, and strive to put his
teachings into practice.*[3]

3 : ZEN

The legendary origins of Zen go back to the Buddha, whose higher, non-verbal teachings were transmitted directly to his disciples, by-passing the head monk.

Zen – Ch'an in Chinese – is really a Chinese development, incorporating elements of the indigenous traditions, notably Taoism. It properly came into its own with the Sixth Patriarch, Hui-neng (638–713 CE), an illiterate who was suddenly enlightened on hearing the *Diamond Sutra* recited while selling firewood. He then went to study at the temple of the Fifth Patriarch, Hung-jen (601–74), and was put to work on the threshing floor. When Hung-jen wished to appoint his successor, he invited his students to show the depth of their understanding by submitting poems. All the monks deferred to the head monk, Shen-hsiu (c600–706), who reluctantly pinned up a poem in which he compared the mind to a bright mirror from which the dust (of thought) had constantly to be wiped. The next night the 'barbarian' from the threshing floor submitted a second poem in which he pointed out that, since the Buddha-nature is always clear and bright, 'where is there room for dust?' This proved to Hung-jen that Hui-neng did indeed possess a deeper understanding of Zen than Shen-hsiu, but he dared not openly confer the transmission on him. He therefore gave him the patriarchal robe privately and told him to leave – quickly.

According to tradition, the rivalry between Hui-neng and Shen-hsiu split Ch'an into two schools. The Southern School of Hui-neng favoured the notion of sudden Enlightenment, while the Northern School of Shen-hsiu favoured the gradual variety. Further subdivisions occurred and subsequently Five Houses and Seven Schools emerged, all propagating the teachings of the Southern School. Of these only two survive today, the Lin-chi and the Ts'ao-tung, which were successfully transmitted to Japan. Zen was also transmitted to Korea, where it is known as Son, and to Vietnam, where it combined with Pure Land in a successful local synthesis.

Classic Chinese Zen (Ch'an)

Very little Chinese Zen remains today. In any case, the golden age of the school was over a millennium ago, during the T'ang dynasty (618–907 CE). Afterwards it became formalized and lost much of its original vitality, though it survived – and indeed more successfully than the other schools – and still occasionally produced an outstanding master, such as Hsü-yün, who, when he died in 1959, was reputed to be 120 years old.

But what was the vintage Ch'an of the T'ang dynasty like?

After centuries of immersion in the teachings brought from India, Chinese Buddhists at last felt confident to make their own unique approach to the core of the Buddha's spiritual project. It was clear that intellectual study could only produce dry head-knowledge, not the direct trans-rational 'un-knowledge' of the heart. So the early masters laid primary emphasis upon direct seeing into the self nature and improvised ingenious ploys to achieve this – shouts and clouts, bizarre behaviour and repartee:

One day as the master [Pai-chang] was walking along with Ma-tsu [his teacher], they saw a flock of wild ducks fly by. The ancestor said, 'What is that?' The master said, 'Wild ducks.' Ma-tsu said, 'Where have they gone?' The master said, 'Flown away.' Ma-tsu then grabbed the master's nose; feeling pain, the master let out a cry. The ancestor said, 'Still you say, "Flown away"?' At these words the master had insight.[4]

This is Enlightenment, not at some indefinite time in the future, but right here, now. For in Ch'an the highest realization is not to be postponed until we are completely purified or have gathered a plethora of scriptural knowledge or clocked up a record-breaking score of meditation hours. To strive for goodness or knowledge, even to seek Enlightenment or to become a buddha, is to pile up further obstructions to attainment. It is like running all over the world looking for a pearl that is fixed to one's forehead.

According to Pai-chang, one is to practise like this:

When things happen, make no response: keep your minds from dwelling on anything whatsoever: keep them for ever still as the void and utterly pure (without stain): and thereby spontaneously attain deliverance.[5]

The field of Zen, therefore, is mind – our own minds; for the One Mind or Buddha Mind and our own minds are not essentially different. According to Pai-chang, 'The nature of mind has no defilement; it is basically perfect and complete in itself.' Our problem is that we sully it with our greed and desire; with discriminative thoughts of good and bad, like and dislike, existence and non-existence; with our concern with past and future – but most of all with our attachments. If we let it all go, mind returns to its native purity, free of obstructions like a shining mirror that can reflect whatever passes into its ambit because it is empty. Precisely this is buddhahood. But it is not to be confused with blank tranquillity. That is yet another trap. Ch'an Enlightenment leans neither towards activity nor to quietude. The mind should abide nowhere and in nothing – not even in not-abiding!

Classic T'ang dynasty Ch'an did not emphasize formal sitting meditation (tso ch'an; Japanese, zazen) as an end in itself. Rather, sitting stilled both mind and body and thereby created the 'inner potentiality' for direct insights to arise in everyday life. Furthermore, many now take the view that the differences between the various subschools were not particularly marked.

OPPOSITE *Sitting in meditation is only one path to Enlightenment and is not an end in itself.*

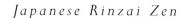

Japanese Soto Zen

T'sao-tung Ch'an was transmitted from China to Japan by Eihei Dogen (1200–53), where it became known as Soto Zen. Dogen attained a Great Enlightenment in China during the summer retreat of 1225, when his teacher, Ju-ching, shouted, 'When you study under a master, you must drop the body and the mind; what is the use of single-minded intense sleeping?' Two years later he returned to Japan 'empty handed' – that is, not bearing scriptures or relics but being himself a living exemplar of the Buddha's teaching. Having been advised by Ju-ching to live in steep mountains and dark valleys, avoiding cities and villages, and not to approach rulers or ministers, Dogen likewise urged his own followers to drop the pursuit of wealth and fame, those perennial hindrances to the spiritual life, and instead to dedicate themselves wholeheartedly to practice.

Central to Dogen's teaching is the importance of intensive sitting meditation and the notion that we are not potentially but *actually* buddhas when we sit. Practice and realization are one and immediate. Implicit in this is rejection of the notion that in the current dark age realization is impossible. He also evolved some original ideas of his own, notably that the Buddha-nature is not beyond impermanence, it *is* impermanence. And, finally, though he taught both monks and laity, men and women, he believed very strongly in a sound monastic basis and worked hard to create that.

Japanese Rinzai Zen

Lin-chi Ch'an was transmitted to Japan, where it became known as Rinzai Zen, by Myoan Eisai (1141–1215). Like Dogen, who came after him, when Eisai returned from China he ran into trouble with the powerful Tendai sect, which succeeded in getting the Zen sect prohibited by imperial edict. Unlike Dogen, however, Eisai was prepared to compromise, and both Tendai esotericism and Zen meditation were practised alongside each other in his temples. Though he was in no doubt that Rinzai Zen represented the quintessence of the Buddha's Dharma, Eisai felt its hour had not yet come in Japan. Nevertheless, he laid a foundation upon which subsequent Japanese and Chinese masters could build.

The rising samurai class found Rinzai Zen very much to their liking, and a dynamic 'on-the-instant' warrior Zen evolved in Kamakura, which used, not the classical formalized koan riddles, but ones improvised on the spot using an incident or situation with which the trainee was familiar. What, for instance, might a samurai do if, while getting naked into his bath, he found himself surrounded by a hundred armed enemies? Would he beg for mercy or die fighting? How might he manage to win without surrendering or fighting?

After an initial period of vitality, Japanese Buddhism went into a long decline. Because it enjoyed the favour of the Shogunate, the Rinzai Zen sect survived most successfully of all the schools, and during the fourteenth and fifteenth centuries lavishly endowed temples flourished, notably the so-called Five Mountains in Kyoto, which are extensive complexes adorned with the finest works of art. Such places fostered that high aesthetic refinement we tend to associate with the Zen arts. But overall the drift both then and thereafter was towards institutionalization, formalization and state regulation, and down to modern times there was little in the way of significant innovation or development, except in the lives and works of two Zen masters, Bankei Yotaku and Hakuin Zenji.

Bankei Yotaku

Bankei Yotaku (1622–93) was one of those rare spirits who have the courage to find their own unique spiritual path, even if it means bucking against some of the hallowed conventions.

His teaching sparkles with originality, and it was certainly highly effective in his own day, for huge crowds drawn from many different persuasions came to hear his discourses. At a time when Zen had become an élite preserve requiring command of classical Chinese and other recherché talents, Bankei was able to transmit its essence to ordinary people in terms that they found accessible. He also had a great gift for inspiring his listeners with confidence in their own spiritual potentiality. Bankei even addressed 'mere women', telling them that they too possessed the Buddha Mind just as men did.

He does not seem to have thought very highly of formal practice: he talks disparagingly of 'device Zen' that depends upon techniques. The monks in his monasteries did meditate – presumably they had to do something! – but he did not lay heavy obligations or rules on them. The important thing is to discover the Unborn, the 'not-become, not-compounded' that the sutra mention, the 'pure shining mind' of the Zen Masters.

This can be done simply and directly, even by lay people. The trick is then to remain with it amidst the hurly-burly of everyday life. If thoughts arise, they should neither be suppressed nor indulged. For to be caught by them is to exchange the Unborn Buddha Mind for that of a fighting demon, a hungry ghost or some other tormented victim of bad karma. One should just remain detached and see that thoughts are transient illusions with no real substance. They will surely pass, leaving only the shining Unborn Buddha Mind – and in the marvellous, effortless functioning of this one can have complete confidence.

Hakuin Zenji

Hakuin Zenji (1686–1769) was a completely contrasting character to Bankei Yotaku. Hakuin never lost faith in the rigours and austerities of hard practice and underwent them fully himself. There was, however, a less severe, aesthetic side to his nature that expressed itself through the Zen arts of calligraphy, painting and poetry. He was also concerned with propagating Buddhism among ordinary people, and in this context he was prepared to relax a little and make a few concessions to human frailty.

Hakuin is now generally regarded as the revitalizer and reformer of the Rinzai system of training, and his influence, unlike that of Bankei, has been a lasting one. In particular he revised and extended the koan system, organizing it into a strict programme of formal study.

Korean Zen (Son)

ABOVE *An ancient Zen temple in South Korea.*

RIGHT *A woodcut by Hasuko (Mrs Christmas Humphreys) of the famous koan 'The sound of one hand clapping'.*

The characteristics of Korean Zen are rather different from those of the Japanese variety. It is both less martial and formal, and a little more earthy. Nuns have their own nunneries, and their status is not materially lower than that of the monks. Generally, Son preserves something of the flavour of classic Ch'an and, in a limited way, has been transmitted to the modern West.

Korean monastic practice incorporates three main elements: study, meditation (Son) and chanting (a Pure Land element). There are separate halls for each of these activities in the monasteries, and monks or nuns are free to specialize in whichever they find most conducive. Study focuses mainly on the Zen records and Mahayana sutras, chanting on the repetition of the names of the Buddha and the Bodhisattvas, and meditation on sitting and koan or hwadu practice. Usually a monk or nun will work on one hwadu, a koan-like question, throughout their training, most probably the ultimate riddle: 'What is it?' Monks and nuns come together for two three-month meditation retreats in the winter and summer seasons.

Western Zen

For most of this century there has been a two-way traffic of Westerners going to Japan to study Zen and Japanese teachers coming to the West. The result is that both the Japanese Rinzai and Soto traditions have been transmitted here and numerous centres established.

The emphasis in Western centres has been mainly on promoting lay practice, though in some the forms of Japanese monasticism, or quasi-monasticism with married 'monks' and 'nuns', have been established. Everywhere, however, the centre of activity is the zendo or meditation hall, which is usually a model of Japanese-style order and simplicity, with a shrine at the far end and neat rows of zafus or meditation cushions facing each other across an empty central aisle. It is here that regular sittings take place, and periods of intensive retreat known as sesshin. Following tradition, Soto students sit facing the wall and engage in their 'just sitting' practice, while Rinzai students face each other and, if so instructed by their teacher, engage in koan study. From time to time an official may march around the

room, carrying a stick known as a keisaku. Those meditators who are becoming drowsy or losing muscle-tone may ask to be struck smartly on the shoulder muscles with this. There is likely to be chanting too, the rhythm beaten out on a mokugyo or 'wooden fish'; also much bowing and impersonal formality. Everything is regulated by strict rules, and this lends the atmosphere an edge of severity and purposefulness.

Because of the traditions of direct transmission and lineage, the Zen master or teacher – who may bear the title roshi ('old master') – continues to be of central importance in Western Zen. Students should have regular interviews with him (or her) and during the course of these a fairly intense relationship may be built up. Ideally a teacher should be able to read how students are progressing, note their blockages and guide-push them forwards. A sizeable amount of power is, of course, invested in this role.

ABOVE *A nun in a monastery in Los Angeles with a keisaku (correction stick) used, at the request of the meditator, to prevent sleep.*

LEFT *A novice monk and his tutor in Bhutan.*

4 : PURE LAND

Shakyamuni Buddha is said to have saved himself 'by his own efforts alone', and this streak of spiritual self-help runs right through Buddhism. You will still hear people today saying, 'You have to do it for yourself – no one else can do it for you,' which is correct, but not altogether true. For faith and devotion perennially arise within the human heart, faith signifying belief that an external agency can help the individual spiritually, and devotion a deep gratitude for the source of that help. There have been such elements in Buddhism from the earliest times. To practise within the Buddhist tradition is in fact to display faith (though hopefully not blind faith) in that tradition. To bow before an image of a buddha or bodhisattva, a teacher or a monk or nun is to show both faith and devotion. So is to light incense, to copy or recite the scriptures, to carve images, to endow temples and monasteries, to feed the Sangha, and so on. Such tendencies grew as the religion itself developed, particularly during the Mahayana phase of its development.

An important early devotional practice was that of Buddhanusmrti or 'Recollection of the Buddha'. This is done by bringing the Buddha to mind, reciting his name, and by visualizing his image and/or his Pure Land or field of activity, which might be either a physical or a transcendental 'place' depending upon the sophistication of the individual view. It is also possible to go beyond recollection of the Buddha as a physical being to a more formless kind of recollection. The benefits to be derived from such practices are considerable. One might have a vision of the Buddha, or attain profound meditative states.

With the rise of the Mahayana we find the emergence of a number of cults of divine buddhas and bodhisattvas, such as Avalalokiteshvara, Mañjushri, Maitreya and Kshitigarbha. Each has his or her own Pure Land. Those drawn to these cults will recollect and worship these divinities in various ways, and pray for them to intercede spiritually on their behalf.

Chinese Pure Land – Ching T'u

Though the devotional strand in Buddhism was just one strand alongside others, a separate tendency did establish itself and a distinct school eventually emerged. This was the Pure Land school, which grew out of the cult of Amitabha, the Buddha of Infinite Light.

The school, which reached its full flowering in China, is based on the legend, recorded in the *Larger Sukhavati-vyuha Sutra*, of an ultra-bodhisattvic monk named Dharmakara, later to become the buddha Amitayus ('Infinite Life' – an aspect of Amitabha), who vowed to create a Pure Land of peerless splendour and not accept Supreme Enlightenment until all sentient beings so wishing had been reborn there. The pious dead would emerge from lotus buds into this Pure Land, the Western Paradise of Sukhavati, where all defilements would be rapidly expunged and Nirvana attained in just one more lifetime.

This legend inspired pious Chinese Pure Landers to be in the best frame of mind at the moment of death in order to proceed smoothly to Sukhavati. Many chose their hour of death in advance, took a bath, lit incense and sat upright to await the end, well secluded from grieving relations who might upset their state of mind. But was this Sukhavati a 'real place', a heaven with tangible features and adornments, or a metaphor for Enlightenment itself? This would again depend upon the sophistication of the individual view.

Also important to Pure Land is the old Buddhist myth of the 'Last Days of the Dharma' (Japanese, Mappo), which maintains that, after an initial period of vitality, the Buddha-dharma will enter a declining phase and finally a long dark age will set in when conditions will be so inimical that it will be impossible to achieve anything by one's own spiritual efforts alone. All one can do is throw oneself upon the mercy of a benign buddha like Amitayus-Amitabha.

Throughout its history Buddhism has tended to be the preserve of the members of an intellectual, spiritual and social élite, and the focus has almost everywhere been in the monasteries. Pure Land Buddhism, however, has more general appeal. It offers an 'easy practice' that can be implemented in the world, without becoming a monk or nun; and it promises salvation to everyone through Amitabha's vows – to those still entrammelled in the passions, even to those who have committed serious crimes. Profound study and meditation are moreover distrusted as they are seen as leading to intellectual and spiritual arrogance.

Pure Land was therefore the first really democratic form of Buddhism, stressing humility rather than attainment, and as such became hugely successful among ordinary Chinese. Pious societies were spawned under its auspices, such as the White Lotus Society, which developed into a sizeable property-owning movement before eventually being suppressed. In its heyday, the good works of its devotees included providing public amenities (bath-houses, hostels, mills, etc.), donating cloth, copying sutras and hosting vegetarian banquets. It was unusual in having married clergy and allowing women to play a prominent part in its affairs.

Of the various schools that burgeoned in T'ang dynasty China, only Pure Land and Ch'an (Zen) had the vitality to survive the great persecution of 845. Indeed, in China the methods of both schools were often practised in tandem for double effectiveness – 'like a tiger wearing horns'.

LEFT *A tanka of the Shakyamuni Buddha surrounded by various deities.*

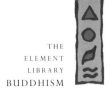

Japanese Pure Land

Once transmitted to Japan, Pure Land became
concentrated and simplified: the remaining
vestiges of Self Power, including residues of
'hard practice', were stripped away, and
primary importance placed upon the
Nembutsu (the recitation of the name of
Amitabha, known in Japan as Amida, in the
formula Namu Amida Butsu), and ultimately
on pure faith and grace. Its propagation was
helped by the fact that the grim Pure Land
world-view of Mappo resonated with the
social realities of Japanese life at the end of the
Heian Era and the beginning of the Kamakura.
Civil strife, famine, disease, pillage, social
breakdown and other evils made ordinary
people very receptive to the notion that they
were living in degenerate times and so were in
need of some special method (or non-method)
of salvation.

Two figures are of particular importance in
Japanese Pure Land: Honen Shonin
(1133–1212), founder of the Jodo-shu ('Pure
Land School'), and his disciple, Shinran
Shonin (1173–1262), founder of the Jodo
Shin-shu ('True Pure Land School').

There is a tendency in the West for Pure
Land Buddhism to be down-graded as a low-
level spiritual path; it is seen as a kind of
Buddho-Christianity for simple souls

Honen Shonin

As a Tendai monk, Honen was sincere and dedicated, but he gradually
became convinced that he lived in a fallen age and despaired of making
any spiritual progress. Only the 'easy practice' of the Nembutsu
possessed any efficacy, he felt. Even one utterance was sufficient to
ensure salvation, though continuous recitation was a healthy discipline,
keeping the mind centred on the ultimate goal. In 1175 Honen left the
Tendai school and began to teach according to his own convictions. A
highly respected and effective monk, he attracted large followings, but
this provoked the jealousy of other sects, who eventually managed to get
his movement suppressed and Honen exiled. He was allowed to return to
the capital in 1211, a year before his death.

Honen is not regarded as an innovator, but he did lay the foundation
for an independent Pure Land movement in Japan.

Shinran Shonin

Shinran, like Honen, served an early spiritual apprenticeship as a Tendai monk, and his efforts again merely led to frustration and conflict. Later, he met Honen, embraced the Pure Land teachings and was banished along with Honen in 1207 and married in exile. He rejected the dichotomy of lay life and monastic life, and propounded the view that passions, far from needing to be expunged, are necessary to salvation. In 1211, he too was pardoned and later went with his family to preach in the Kanto area, where he attracted a considerable following.

Shinran probed deeper than Honen and came to the conclusion that the actual recitation of the Nembutsu is not as important as the underlying quality of faith, which he equated with the Buddha-nature itself.

Faith cannot, however, be contrived by an effort of will but by pure grace – a gift bestowed by Amida, whom Shinran regarded as the ultimate Buddha. In receiving this gift of faith, one feels enormous gratitude and can accept oneself totally, vices and all, for one is saved in spite of them.

incapable of shaping up to the demands of, say, Zen or Tantric practice. This is a misrepresentation. What Pure Land is saying is that we must let go of all self-initiated activity, have complete faith in the Buddha-nature within and allow it to function in its own mysterious way without interference from the thinking mind. In this way it is not very different from Zen – or other forms of Buddhism. The Nembutsu concentrates and clears the mind, and focuses on the Buddha-nature within.

The Pure Land schools of Honen and Shinran survive to this day, and have been highly successful at the popular level in Japan. They still eschew monasticism, concentrating on a simple theology of faith and Nembutsu practice that can be applied in everyday life. Though championed by important pioneer Buddhist writers such as D T Suzuki and Alan Watts, Japanese Pure Land Buddhism has not transplanted successfully in the West. Suzuki thought that Shin Buddhism might one day prove to be Asia's greatest gift to the West, while Watts was drawn to the Shin teaching of self-acceptance and the notion that we are saved as we are, warts and all. Such notions contain inherent problems, however, for if we are saved as we are, why bother to improve ourselves spiritually or attempt to lead moral lives?

OPPOSITE *Myde Shonin, a descendant of the Pure Land Founders, exemplifying the practice of communing with nature.*

BELOW LEFT *This ink drawing of a circle by Zen Master Singai represents both the totality of the Universe and its ultimate emptiness.*

BELOW *Japanese monks on Mount Koyasan, near Osaka, bow to one another in the traditional sign of respect.*

5: NICHIREN

text's title encapsulated the totality of truth in the Universe and as such was an embodiment of Shakyamuni Buddha. As a practice, therefore, Nichiren prescribed the Daimoku or chanting of the formula Namu-myoho-renge-kyo – 'Homage to the Lotus Sutra of the True Law'.

Nichiren started to proselytize in 1253 – and from the start there was a strong political dimension to his work. He not only unrelentingly denounced the other schools – he regarded this as a religious practice in itself – but also called upon the authorities to suppress them. All the natural and social calamities of the time stemmed from failure to embrace the *Lotus Sutra* and toleration of

There is much talk nowadays of Buddhism as 'the fastest growing religion in the West'. Ironically, the brand of Buddhism attracting the largest number of new followers is regarded by many as the least representatively Buddhist of all the schools. This is the Nichiren Sho-shu or 'True Nichiren School', the most successful of the various subschools that trace their roots back to Kamakura Era Japan and a Tendai monk named Nichiren Shonin (1222–82). Today, Nichiren Sho-shu propagates an attractive form of 'Designer Buddhism' with an uncomplicated central chanting practice that draws pop and soap opera stars, fashion and media operators – and hordes of mainly young people.

Nichiren himself was a product of the same fraught milieu as Honen and Shinran. Like them, he became convinced that he was living in the degenerate age of Mappo, but, having been ordained into the Tendai school, he believed that the *Lotus Sutra* embodies the true teachings of Shakyamuni Buddha and that complete faith in it is the sole key to salvation. Other Buddhist schools, he came to believe, did not merely disseminate futile teachings and practices; they were downright pernicious insofar as they diverted people from the One True Path. Not that one had to study deeply and reflect upon the *Lotus Sutra*, however. The

heterodox schools, he declared. And in 1268, when a Mongol invasion threatened, he warned that only faith in the *Lotus* could save Japan. Such aggressive outspokenness naturally alienated the other schools.

Schisms arose within the Nichiren school after the founder's death, one cause of controversy being relations with other schools. Some groupings favoured a more moderate approach, while others advocated the hard line of 'neither to receive nor to give' (fujufuse). Nichiren Sho-shu is definitely of the latter, tracing its spiritual roots back to a thirteenth-century hard-liner named Nikko, although actually founded in 1937 by a pragmatic educator named Tsunesaburo Makiguchi (1871–1944). As a movement with the alternative title of Soka Gakkai ('Value Creating Society') it burgeoned along with other 'new religions' after the military defeat of 1945, when the Japanese suffered a grave collective trauma. Its first leader during the postwar period was Josei Toda (1900–58), who promoted it so successfully (if controversially) that by 1960 it could claim the loyalty of 750,000 households. Toda was succeeded by Daisaku Ikeda (b.1928), who founded a political party, the Komeito ('Clean Government Party'). This has since had to sever its connections with Soka Gakkai.

Nichiren Sho-shu teaches that our destiny lies in our own hands. We must take responsibility for our own lives and make the necessary positive moves to settle our problems and realize our full potential. To these ends, members are actively counselled, helped and supported by the movement, and are encouraged to take up a three-fold practice involving faith, study and chanting. Faith is faith in the power of Gohonzon, a scroll on which Namu-myoho-renge-kyo is written in mandalic form. The original, penned by Nichiren himself, is lodged in the head temple of Taiseki-ji at the foot of Mount Fuji, but members obtain their own copy and perform Gongyo before it twice daily. Gongyo involves chanting Namu-myoho-renge-kyo, plus selected passages from the *Lotus Sutra*. Finally, there is study of the Buddhist teachings as reformulated by

Nichiren and his successors. All this can be carried out without renouncing the world. Indeed, worldly success is valued within Nichiren Sho-shu, though it is also taught that it cannot lead to lasting happiness. That is only possible by sublimating the lower energies to higher purposes.

Currently, Nichiren Sho-shu is unique in avoiding relations with other Buddhist groups. It still affirms that Nichiren's teachings, which it describes as 'revolutionary' and hence difficult for many other Buddhists to accept, are uniquely suitable for our time. Nichiren himself was, as we have seen, never loath to stir up controversy and hot emotions. He thought them creative forces. Following the founder, therefore, Nichiren Sho-shu maintains the old tradition of shakubuku or vigorous proselytizing.

Other Nichiren subschools that have been brought to the West, albeit less successfully than Nichiren Sho-shu, include Reiyukai and its off-shoot Rissho Koseikai; also the Nipponzan Myohoji order founded by Nichidatsu Fujii (1885–1985), a man deeply influenced by Mahatma Gandhi. His white-robed monks and nuns have built peace pagodas in many parts of the world, and otherwise work tirelessly and harmoniously with other groups to promote world peace.

OPPOSITE ABOVE
The Golden Pagoda in Kyoto, Japan.

OPPOSITE BELOW
The London Peace Pagoda, a shrine of peace, was a gift from the Japanese government to the people of Britain. More and more people in the West are being drawn to the peaceful, non-violent spirit of the Buddhist philosophy.

ABOVE *Japanese guests at the London Peace Pagoda.*

ENDWORD:
GOING FURTHER

The Spiritual Search

Many approach Buddhism out of purely intellectual curiosity, but others will want to go further and know it more deeply. The spiritual search to find out who we really are is the greatest adventure. It is the quest for the Holy Grail, for the pearl of great price. Often we have to be driven out of our complacency to embark on this spiritual quest. A devastating crisis, much suffering, or a growing tiredness of going round and round, repeating the same increasingly meaningless patterns: these are the most common precipitating factors. The main problem that besets the person interested in going further is not difficulty in obtaining teaching, but rather the embarrassment of too much choice. We are in a fortunate position. Because all the major Buddhist schools and traditions have now been transmitted to the West, we can have a much clearer view of what is on offer. We can therefore allow ourselves to experiment in order to find out what suits us best. At some point one usually has to make a commitment to a particular course of study and practice, but it is best not to hurry the process. Commitment will generally arise quite naturally of its own accord when a situation feels right, whereas forcing the issue can lead to trouble.

Practice and Learning

Once committed, guard against running away. When Buddhism really begins to 'work', things often get difficult – sometimes very difficult. One may, for instance, have to face inner truths that one has been dodging for years. The ego does not open itself to new growth without a struggle. On the other hand, do not feel afraid to leave a group or teacher when it is clear that they have ceased to work for you. Always, however, be watchful – delve into your own motivations, check your responses and feelings, and keep a clear eye on what is happening around you, avoiding the extremes of being a destructive critic or a starry-eyed innocent. The Buddhist Way is the middle way – and it is all about learning.

Always be realistic and do not fall prey to illusions. Remember that religious people and institutions are much like worldly ones. They have their dark as well as their light sides. Do not be too dazzled by charismatic teachers, or ones with mass followings, or great fame, power or worldly wealth. Be careful too of teachers and groups that pressure you for money or services.

We go to teachers and groups at the beginning because we need information, guidance and the support of like-minded people. But always the main aim in Buddhism is to help the individual to become free, autonomous, self-reliant. The teacher or group that helps you achieve this is therefore healthy and right-directed. Always maintain a centre of strength and self-reliance within yourself. Do not be pressured out of it.

A word about the ego. The old 'I' is relentlessly blamed for all our own and the world's woes. In fact the ego is only problematic if its development has been stultified or if there is exclusive clinging to it. A healthy, stable ego, on the other hand, is an absolute necessity for successful functioning in the world. Without this, higher spiritual development cannot be safely undertaken and one can get stuck in all kinds of negative states, perhaps suffering much psychological pain – and certainly never fulfilling one's potential. Part of one's work may therefore be to heal old wounds. In this context many seekers have found the modern Western psychotherapies very useful. Once that is realized, however, 'trans-egoic' development may begin – that is, opening to that which is beyond 'me'.

Difficulties and Dangers

If the spiritual quest is a great adventure, it must have its difficulties and dangers. Nothing worthwhile is ever achieved by staying at home in safety and comfort. One has to throw oneself into the unknown and brave its mysteries. There are many pitfalls on the path, some of which we touched on above, but the greatest of all is spiritual inflation. This is a dire condition in which the ego is enlarged, blown up like a balloon. Gurus and teachers are particularly vulnerable to this, for they enjoy power, prestige and public acclaim and so are very susceptible to corruption. Watch out for the presence of the power complex: this often goes with a certain ruthlessness and contempt for the well-being of others, as though they are of no account and so can be used and abused at will. Every practitioner, however, even the beginner, should be vigilant at all times. This is the basic safeguard and must be kept up, particularly at times when things seem to be going well and one thinks one is 'making progress'.

Do not use Buddhism as an escape from the world or the problems of social living. It is easy to get hooked on a kind of 'Ivory Tower Buddhism', where the rest of the world can go hang while you concentrate on the great task of your own spiritual salvation. The Buddha himself, when occasion demanded, was never reluctant to intervene in social situations, and he even made political pronouncements.

Do not expect too much of yourself at the beginning. Real and lasting change is a long, slow business. Practise regularly and conscientiously, but do not become some kind of spiritual athlete trying to break records. In the same way, do not turn your practice into a kind of penance. We often suffer from deep-seated guilts and self-hatred. Because of this, we are hard on ourselves – and hard on others too. What we really need is to soften up, to open our hearts and allow our innate but stifled warmth to emerge. This is very much what Buddhist practice is about, especially the

Mahayana variety with its primary emphasis on compassion. There are forms of Buddhist practice that are very harsh. While those may have been appropriate in the areas and situations in which they were originally developed, it is doubtful whether they are always beneficial for hard-nosed Westerners, who often need more of the opposite treatment.

BELOW *Female novice
nuns in Burma.*

OVERLEAF *An
eighteenth-century
painting of the Buddha's
disciple Wu Laing-shan.*

The Buddhist Path

While being aware of the pitfalls of the path, do not be deterred by them. Always try to remain open. You cannot learn if you are not open – and open-minded. You never know from which unlikely direction your next important teaching is going to come. Openness means being fully alert and aware, not blocking anything out, not avoiding things (especially unpleasant things). It means letting go of the need to control. However, be realistic too; do not continue to be open when it is clear it is no longer sensible to do so. Openness is not synonymous with naiveté or gullibility. The middle way again …

This is in many ways a good time to explore Buddhism. Any spiritual tradition has a lot of the true spirit in it when it is new or undergoing a new phase of development, as Buddhism is in its expansion in the West. Before too long the infrastructure of an organized 'church' will no doubt emerge (in fact we are seeing the beginnings of this) and, as we know from past experience, churches nearly always suppress that anarchic spiritual tradition that places primary emphasis on direct mystical insight – on seeing the truth for oneself. The function of authentic spirituality is not to provide security and solace but to encourage the seeker to venture out on the lonely and difficult path of self-knowledge.

So do not be intimidated. Have confidence in your own spiritual potential, your ability to find your own unique way. Learn from others, certainly, and use what you find useful, but also learn to trust your own inner wisdom. Have courage. Be awake and aware. Remember too that Buddhism is not about being 'a Buddhist'. Nor is it about collecting head-knowledge, practices and techniques. It is ultimately about letting go of all forms and concepts and becoming free.

So be prepared to cut through all superfluous accretions and go for the gold of the spiritual core. It is certainly there, and, so the greatest Buddhist masters assure us, is not as difficult to get at as we often tend to think.

NOTES AND REFERENCES

Introduction

1 The question is often asked by modern Western Buddhists whether these realms, especially the hell realms, are 'real' or metaphors for psychological states. In the Buddhist scriptures they are certainly depicted as real and the faithful of traditional Buddhist countries certainly regard them as such. However, this does not settle the matter. Religious teachers and writers have often resorted to creating lurid hell realms for pragmatic reasons, in order to discourage their followers from 'evil'.

Chapter 2

1 It is also called by other names: for example, the Mantrayana or Secret Mantra school, though this probably originated at an early phase.
2 'Buddhism in India' by L Gomez, in *The Encyclopaedia of Religion*, vol. 2, ed. M Éliade, New York and London, 1987, p. 377

Chapter 4

1 *The Colossus of Maroussi*, Henry Miller, paperback edition, London, 1950, p. 203
2 *Dhammapada*, chapter 1, verse 1
3 Actually we should not talk of a single consciousness traversing the bardo. It is more like a stream of causally interconnected consciousness moments. We could therefore call it a 'consciousness continuum'.
4 *Majjhima Nikaya*, 245–6

Chapter 5

1 Actually, the notion of Shunyata arose among the Hinayana schools, but it was fully developed in and became one of the benchmarks of the Mahayana.
2 The following is based upon Stephen Batchelor's translation of Shantideva's *Bodhisattvacharyavatara*, reprinted, Library of Tibetan Works & Archives, Dharamsala, 1987.
3 *The Short Prajñaparamita Texts*, trans. E Conze, London, 1973, p. 138

Chapter 6

1 *Idle Jottings*, Zen Reflections from the Tsure-zure Gusa of Yoshida Kenko, ed. Irwin Switzer III, Totnes, 1988, p. 36

Chapter 7

1 'Satipatthana Sutta' from Vol. 1 of the *Majjhima Nikaya*, trans. I B Horner, Reprinted Leicester, 1988, pp. 5–6
2 *Buddhist Dictionary*, Ven. Nyanatiloka, revised and enlarged edition, Kandy, 1972, p. 44

3 '*Madhyantavibhagabhasya*', Vasubandhu, Chapter 4, trans. Stefan Anacker in *Mahayana Buddhist Meditation*, ed. M Kiyota, Honolulu, 1978, pp. 106–7, p. 91
4 'Rules for Zazen' (Zazen-gi) trans. D Welch and K Tanahashi, in *Moon in a Dewdrop: Writings of Zen Master Dogen*, ed. K Tanahashi, UK edition Shaftesbury, 1988, p. 30

Chapter 8

1 The suffix -*pa* denotes a person. Thus a Nyingmapa is a person who adheres to the Nyingma school. The Western plural form -*pas*, now in popular use, denotes a quantity of people, or in this case the followers of the school.
2 Introduction to *The History of the Sakya Tradition*, by Chogay Trichen, Bristol, 1983, p. x
3 *The Jewelled Staircase*, by Geshe Wangyal, Ithaca, N.Y., 1986, p. 62
4 *The Sayings & Doings of Pai-chang*, trans. Thomas Cleary, Los Angeles, 1978, pp. 18–19
5 *The Zen Teachings of Hui-hai on Instantaneous Enlightenment*, trans. John Blofeld, reprint, Leicester, 1987, p. 49. Blofeld's Hui-hai is the same person as Cleary's Pai-chang

ACKNOWLEDGEMENTS

Archiv für Kunst und Geschichte, London: FINE ARTS MUSEUM, ULAN BATOR 23; STUTTGART LINDEN MUSEUM 30.
Bodleian Library, Oxford: (MS Sansk a.7.(R)) 24t.
The Bridgeman Art Library, London: CHRISTIES 62; ODILON REDON: THE BUDDHA/MUSÉE D'ORSAY/GIRAUDON title page and 32/33; ORIENTAL MUSEUM, DURHAM UNIVERSITY 17, 84; ROYAL GEOGRAPHICAL SOCIETY 74; PRIVATE COLLECTION 60.
British Library: LIFE OF BUDDHA 12, 14/15, 36/37, 40b, 41b.
e.t.archive, London: BRITISH LIBRARY 48/49; BRITISH MUSEUM 52.
Fortean Picture Library, Ruthin: KLAUS AARSLEFF 18.
Michael Holford, London: 47; BRITISH MUSEUM 45.
The Hutchison Library, London: TIM BEDDOW 10; DAVID BRINICOMBE 7, 28; JON BURBANK 6; PIERETTE COLLOMB 31tr; SARAH ERRINGTON 83b; CARLOS FREIRE 21tl, 77, 88tl; MELANIE FRIEND 89; SARAH GILES 63; PATRICIO GOYCOOLEA 58, 61; FELIX GREENE 74/75; JEREMY HORNER 26, 92; RICHARD HOUSE 16; ALAN HUTCHISON 31bl; MICHAEL MACINTYRE 24, 51, 71b, 73m, 79, 83t, 87; PETER MONTAGNON 37tr; TREVOR PAGE 55b; JENNY PATE 19br; CHRISTINE PEMBERTON 65; STEPHEN PERN 76; JACKIE AND ALAN REDITT 82; NIGEL SITWELL 11; DR NIGEL SMITH 59, 64, 73t; IVAN STRASBURG 25tr; LIBA TAYLOR 88.
Images Colour Library, London: 8l, 29, 34, 42, 44, 54, 70.
Impact Photos, London: MOHAMED ANSAR 73b.
Ann and Bury Peerless, Birchinton, Kent: 13, 71t.

GLOSSARY

ABHISHEKA The rite of initiation.
ANATMAN Buddhist teaching that originated as a reaction against the brahmanical concept of atman.
ANITYA Impermanence.
ARHAT The 'noble one', one who is assured of Enlightenment.
ATMAN The soul or self, which according to Brahman teachings is one in reality with Brahman – the ultimate reality.
AVIDYA Delusion, ignorance.
BARDO In Tibetan Buddhism, the intermediate state that intervenes between one life and another.
BHUMI A stage on the Bodhisattva Path.
BUDDHAVACANA The word of Buddha.
BODHICITTA Enlightened mind.
BODHISATTVA One who is motivated by compassionate zeal to help others on the path to their own Enlightenment.

DHARMA The path of liberation, the truth, the way.
DHARMAS The ultimate building blocks of reality.
DHYANA Bliss state, state of trance.
DUHKHA Suffering.
DVESHA Anger, hatred.
KARMA The consequences of one's actions of body, speech and mind.
KARUNA Compassion.
MANDALA Symbolic models of the cosmos.
MANTRA Sacred formulae.
NIRVANA The escape from Samsara (cyclic existence).
PARAMITA Perfected virtue.
PARINIRVANA 'Beyond Nirvana'. The State that one who has reached Nirvana passed into after death.
PRAJÑA Wisdom.
PRAJÑAPARAMITA Perfection of Wisdom.
PRATIMOKSHA Code of rules for monks and nuns.

SAMADHI A state of complete concentration and absorbed contemplation.
SAMSARA The cycle of death and rebirth.
SANGHA A community of Buddhist monks.
SHUNYATA Emptiness.
SIDDHAS Adepts.
SKANDHAS The five basic components that make up the individual person.
SUKHA Pleasant feeling.
TANTRA Mystical and magical Buddhist writings.
TANTRIKA A person who is an adept of Tantra.
TRISHNA Thirst, craving, desire.
UPAYA Skilful means for arriving at direct perception of truth.
VAJRA A Buddhist symbol derived from the mythical thunderbolt of the Indian god Indra.
VIPAKA The fruit which comes from a preceding cause or action.

FURTHER READING

STUDIES

GENERAL
Béchert and Gombrich, ed., *The World of Buddhism*, Thames & Hudson, London, 1985
Snelling, John, *The Buddhist Handbook*, Century-Hutchinson, London, 1987

REFERENCE
The Buddhist Directory, The Buddhist Society, London, 1987
Humphreys, Christmas, *A Popular Dictionary of Buddhism*, Arco, London, 1962
Thera, Nyanatiloka, *Buddhist Dictionary*, Buddhist Publication Society, Kandy, 1980
Zen Buddhism in North America, A History & Directory, Zen Lotus Society, Toronto, 1986

THE BUDDHIST WORLD-VIEW
Kloetzli, R, *Buddhist Cosmology*, Motilal Banarsidass, Delhi, 1983

THE BUDDHA
Ling, Trevor, *The Buddha*, Penguin Books, Harmondsworth, 1973
Ñyanamoli, Bhikkhu, *The Life of the Buddha*, Buddhist Publication Society, Kandy, 1971

MEDITATION
Kiyota, Minoru, *Mahayana Buddhist Meditation: Theory & Practice*, University of Hawaii Press, Honolulu, 1978
Kornfield, Jack, *Living Buddhist Masters*, reprint, Shambhala Publications, Boulder, 1983
Thera, Nyanaponika, *The Heart of Buddhist Meditation*, Rider Books, London, 1962

INDIAN BUDDHISM
Lamotte, É, trans. S Webb-Boin, *History of Indian Buddhism*, Peeters Press, Louvain, 1988
Warder, K, *Indian Buddhism*, Motilal Banarsidass, Delhi, 1970, reprint 1980

THERAVADA BUDDHISM
Gombrich, R, *Theravada Buddhism*, Routledge & Kegal Paul, London, 1988
Rahula, W, *What the Buddha Taught*, Gordon Frazer, Bedford, 1972
Sumedho, Ajahn, *Cittaviveka*, Chithurst Forest Monastery, Petersfield, 1983

MAHAYANA BUDDHISM (GENERAL)
Williams, Paul, *Mahayana Buddhism*, Kegan Paul, London, 1989

VAJRAYANA/TANTRA

See **TIBETAN BUDDHISM** below

BUDDHIST PHILOSOPHY

Cleary, Thomas, *Entry into the Inconceivable: An Introduction to Hua-yen Buddhism*, University of Hawaii Press, Honolulu, 1983

Cook, Francis, *Hua-yen Buddhism: The Jewel Net of Indra*, Pennsylvania State University Press, University Park, 1981

Murti, T R V, *The Central Philosophy of Buddhism*, George Allen & Unwin, London, 1955 (A study of the Madhyamaka system)

Stcherbatsky, T, *The Central Conception of Buddhism (and the Meaning of the World 'Dharma')*, London 1923, reprint Motilal Banarsidass, Delhi, 1970

Suzuki, D T, *Studies in the Lankavatara Sutra*, Routledge, London, 1930

Takakusu, J, *Essentials of Buddhist Philosophy*, reprint Motilal Banarsidass, Delhi, 1975

CHINESE BUDDHISM

Chen, K, *Buddhism in China*, Princeton University Press, Princeton, 1964

Wright, A F, *Buddhism in Chinese History*, Stamford University Press, Stamford, 1965

PURE LAND

Bloom, Alfred, *Shinran's Gospel of Pure Grace*, University of Arizona Press, Tucson, Arizona, 1965, reprint 1981

Hirota, D, trans., *Plain Words on the Pure Land Way*, University, Kyoto, 1989

NICHIREN

Causton, R, *Nichiren Shoshu Buddhism*, Century, London, 1988

CHINESE & JAPANESE ZEN

Aitken, Robert, *Taking the Path of Zen*, North Point Press, San Francisco, 1982

Dumoulin, H, *A History of Zen Buddhism*, Faber, London, 1968

Leggett, T, *A First Zen Reader*, Charles Tuttle, Tokyo & Rutland, Vermont, 1960

Leggett, T, *Zen & the Ways*, RKP, London, 1978

Luk, C, trans., *Empty Cloud: The Autobiography of Chinese Zen Master Xu Yun*, Element Books, Dorset, 1988

Sato, Giei & Nishimura, Eshin, *Unsui: A Diary of a Zen Monk*, University of Hawaii Press, Honolulu, 1973

KOREAN ZEN

Sunim, Kusan, trans. M Fages, *The Way of Korean Zen*, Weatherhill, New York & Tokyo, 1985

TIBETAN BUDDHISM

Batchelor, S, ed., *The Jewel in the Lotus*, Wisdom Publications, London, 1987

Rabten, Geshe & Dhargyey, Geshe, *Advice from a Spiritual Friend*, Wisdom Publications, London, 1978

Rinpoche, Tulku Thondup, *Hidden Teachings of Tibet*, Wisdom Publications, London, 1986

Rinpoche, Namkhai Norbu, *The Crystal & the Way of Light*, RKP, London, 1986

Tucci, G, *The Religions of Tibet*, RKP, London, 1980

WESTERN BUDDHISM

Fields, R, *How the Swans Came to the Lake*, revised edition, Shambhala, Boston, 1986 (Buddhism in the USA)

Oliver, P, *Buddhism in Britain*, Rider Books, London, 1979

BUDDHISM & WESTERN PSYCHOLOGY

Jung, C G, *Psychology & the East*, RKP, London, 1978.

Katz, Nathan, *Buddhism & Western Psychology*, Shambhala, Boulder, 1983

Watts, Alan, *Psychotherapy East & West*, Ballantine Books, New York, 1961

BUDDHISM & SOCIAL ACTION

Jones, Ken, *The Social Face of Buddhism (An Approach to Social & Political Activism)*, Wisdom Publications, London, 1989

Thich Nhat Hanh, *Being Peace*, Parallax Press, Berkeley, 1987

JOURNALS & BOOK SERVICE

BUDDHIST JOURNALS

Buddhism Now, published by Buddhism Publication Group, Sharpham Coach Yard, Ashprington, Totnes, Devon TQ9 7UT, UK. (Tel: 01803-732082)

Buddhist Studies Review, 31 Russell Chambers, Bury Place, London WC1A 2JX, UK

Buddhist Studies Review, Prof. Charles S Prebish, Penn State University, 108 Weaver Bldg, University Park, PA 16802-5500, USA (Tel: 814-865 1121, Fax: 814-863 7840, E-Mail CSPI @ PSUVM.PSU.EDU)

Inquiring Mind, PO Box 9999, North Berkeley Station, Berkeley, CA 94709, USA

The Middle Way, published by The Buddhist Society, 58 Eccleston Square, London SW1V 1PH, UK. (Tel: 0171-834 5858 between 2–6pm GMT only)

Sangha Newsletter, published by English Sangha Trust, Amaravati Buddhist Monastery, Gt. Gaddesden, Hemel Hempstead, Herts HP1 3BZ, UK (Tel: 01442-842455)

Shambhala Sun, PO Box 399, Halifax, NS, Canada, B3J 2P8 (Tel: 902 422-8404, Fax: 902 423-2750)

Tricycle, the Buddhist Review, 163 West 22nd Street, New York, NY 10011, USA (Tel: 212 645-1143, Fax: 212 645-1493)

BUDDHIST BOOK SERVICES

Wisdom Books
402 Hoe Street,
London E17 9AA.
(Tel: 0181-520 5588)

Wisdom Publications
361 Newbury Street,
Boston, MA 02115, USA.

Mandala Books
620 Camberwell Road,
Camberwell, Victoria
3124, Australia

INDEX

A

Abhidharma Pitaka 19, 37
abisheka 25, 68, 94
alcohol 57
Amitabha 22, 47, 65, 85, 86
anatman 36, 45, 94
anitya 80, 94
arhat 21, 94
atman 45, 94
avidya 8, 94
awareness 57, 58

B

Bankei Yotaku 81
bardo state 41, 68, 93, 94
bhumi 21, 94
Blavatsky, Madame 27, 32
Bodhi (Bo) tree 13, 15, 39
bodhicitta 46, 68, 94
bodhisattva 21–2, 46–7, 65, 94
Buddha 10–17
    death 17, 41
    early years 10, 36
    enlightenment 14–15
    spiritual quest 12–13
    teachings 16–17, 19, 34–43
Buddhavacana 19, 94
Buddhism
    Hinayana 18–19, 93
    Mahayana 18–23, 44–53
    origins 6–9
    schools/traditions 70–89
    Tantric 24, 27, 31, 56, 68
    Theravada 27, 33, 55, 71–3
    Tibet 31, 33, 41, 50, 74–7
    transmissions 26–33
    Vajrayana 24–5
Burma 27, 71

C

Calm Abiding 61, 64, 68
chakras 68, 69
Ch'an see Zen
change 42, 44
China 28–9, 78, 79, 85
compassion 21, 42, 46–7, 64, 68
consciousness 50
cyclic creation 7, 38

D

Daimoku 88, 89
Dalai Lama 74, 76, 77
death 7, 8, 40, 85
delusion 8, 24, 36
Dependent Origination 14, 38
desire 42
destinations 7, 17, 41
Dharma 15, 17, 18, 85, 94
dharmas 37, 45, 94
dhutanga 72, 81, 86
dhyana 8, 21, 61, 94
Diamond Sutra 49, 78
diet 55, 57, 72
Dogen, Eihei 67, 80
drugs 57
duhkha 35, 94
dvesha 8

E

ego 36, 42, 90
Eight Precepts 72
Eisai, Myoan 80
emptiness 45, 65, 68, 93, 94
Enlightenment 8, 14
    Mahayana 20, 46, 49
    Sakya school 75
    Tantra 24, 25, 56, 68
    Zen 78, 79
environment 57
equanimity 64
Europe 32, 72, 87

F

Five Precepts 55–7, 72, 73
Flower Adornment school 53, 57

G

Gelug school 76

H

Hakuin Zenji 81
hard practice 71, 72, 81, 86
Heart Sutra 49
Heavenly Abodes 64
Hinayana 18–19, 93
Honen Shonin 86
Hua-Yen school 53, 57
Hui-neng school 78

I

'I' 36, 47, 90
impermanence 42, 80, 94
India 6, 18–25
individualism 33
Indonesia 11, 27, 51
insight 61, 65, 68

J

Japan 30, 53, 78
    Nichiren school 88–9
    Pure Land 86
    Zen 80, 83

K

Kagyu school 76
Kampuchea 27
karma 7, 14, 39, 47, 94
karuna 21, 46, 64, 94
killing 55
koan 67, 80, 81, 82, 83
Korea 29, 78, 82

L

lama 33, 74, 76, 77
Laos 27
liberation 8, 12, 15
Lin-chi Ch'an 30, 67, 78, 80, 81, 83
Lotus Sutra 65, 88

M

Madhyamaka 50
magic 24, 25, 75, 76
Mahayana 18–23, 27, 44–53, 65, 74, 84

mandala 9, 24, 68, 94
Mañjushri 22, 74
mantra 24, 68, 94
meditation 6, 22, 58–69
    basics 62
    Buddha 12, 13
    loving-kindness 64
    Mahayana 65
    Tantric 68
    Zen 67, 79, 80, 83
middle way 37, 50
mindfulness 59, 65, 68
monasteries 16, 25, 29, 30, 31
    Theravada 27, 72–3
    Zen 53
monks 16, 33, 55, 71–3
morality 54–7
Myanmar 27

N

nadi 68, 69
Nagarjuna 20, 50
Nembutsu 86, 87
Nichiren Sho-shu 30, 88–9
Nirvana 8, 14, 43, 94
    Mahayana 21, 49
    meditation 61
    Sakya school 75
'not-self' 36, 45
nuns 72, 82
Nyingma school 75

P

Pali Canon 19, 55, 71
Pancha Sila 55, 73
paramita 21, 94
Parinirvarna 17, 43, 94
prajña 21, 94
Prajñaparamita 20, 24, 49, 94
Pratimoksha 16, 94
Pure Land 29, 32, 78, 84–7

R

realms 7, 41, 93
rebirth 7, 8, 40–1
riddles 67, 80, 81, 82
Right Livelihood 57
Rinzai Zen 30, 67, 78, 80, 81, 83
rules 16, 55–7, 71, 72, 83

S

Sakya school 75
samadhi 65, 94
samapattis 61
Samsara 8, 14, 49, 65, 75, 94
Sangha 16, 94
self 45, 47, 86, 87
sex 56
Shamatha 61, 64, 65, 68
Shen-hsiu school 78
Shinran Shonin 86, 87
Shunyata 45, 65, 68, 93, 94
Siddhartha Gautama see Buddha
siddhas 25, 94
siddhis 61
skandhas 36–7

social action 33
Son 82
Soto Zen 67, 78, 80, 83
speech 56
Sri Lanka 27, 71
suffering 35, 65
sukha 35, 94
Sutra Pitaka 19
Sutra traditions 25, 31, 49

T

tantra 94
Tantric Buddhism 24–5, 27
    meditation 68
    morality 56, 57
    Tibet 31, 74, 75
tantrika 24, 25, 94
Tendai school 53, 65, 86–8
Thailand 27, 71
theft 55
Theosophy 27, 32
Theravada 27, 33, 55, 71–3
Three Baskets 19
Three Fires/Poisons 8
Three Refuges 29
Tibet 31, 33, 41, 50, 74–7
T'ien-t'ai school 53, 65, 86–8
trance states 61
transmission, Buddhism 26–33
Tripitaka see Pali Canon
trishna 8, 94
truth 9, 34, 56, 88
Ts'ao-tung school 78, 80

U

United States 32, 87
upaya 21, 22, 34, 94
Uposatha days 72, 73

V

vajra 94
Vajrapani 23, 74
Vajrayana 24–5, 31
Vietnam 29, 78
Viharas 64
Vijñañavada school 50
Vinaya Pitaka 19, 33, 55
vipaka 7, 94
Vipashyana 61, 65, 68

W

Western Buddhism 9, 32–3, 74, 83, 88, 90, 92
wheel of life 8, 14
White Lotus school 53, 85–8
wisdom 21, 34, 42, 49, 65
women 33, 72, 81, 82, 85

Y

yoga 6, 24, 50
Yogacara 50, 65

Z

zazen 67, 93
Zen 29, 30, 32, 53, 67, 78–83